A HANDBOOK FOR
BEGINNING
CHORAL
EDUCATORS

A HANDBOOK FOR
BEGINNING
CHORAL
EDUCATORS

Walter Lamble

INDIANA UNIVERSITY PRESS
Bloomington and Indianapolis

This book is a publication of

Indiana University Press
601 North Morton Street
Bloomington, IN 47404-3797 USA

http://iupress.indiana.edu

Telephone orders	800-842-6796
Fax orders	812-855-7931
Orders by e-mail	iuporder@indiana.edu

The paper used in this publication meets the minimum requirements of
American National Standard for Information Sciences—Permanence of
Paper for Printed Library Materials, ANSI Z39.48-1984.

Manufactured in the United States of America

Library of Congress Cataloging-in-Publication Data

Lamble, Walter, date
   A handbook for beginning choral educators / Walter Lamble.
      p. cm.
   Includes index.
   ISBN 0–253-34434–4 (cloth : alk. paper)—ISBN 0–253-21698–2
(pbk. : alk. paper)
      1. Choral music—Instruction and study. I. Title.
   MT875.L35 2004
   782.5'071—dc22

                                                            2004000690

1 2 3 4 5 09 08 07 06 05 04

CONTENTS

PREFACE

When I realized that retirement was near, after thirty-plus years teaching choral music in the public schools, I had this great idea of staying an extra half hour or so each day after school to build a sort of journal in which I discussed the activities of the day—its problems and solutions.

The journal plan lasted about a week before I quit making daily entries. Soon I gave up completely. But after I retired, I still wanted to get a lot of thoughts on paper to help someone new to the profession.

Sometimes I have written plain facts, things that everyone should know. A lot of the time I write my opinions, based on my years of experience teaching in the public schools. There will undoubtedly be directors who did things differently than I to great effect. I hope I have made no out-and-out errors of fact during the writing of this work. But these are my experiences.

I have a wish for every young teacher (and any veterans, as well). I hope that each of you has the terrific experience I had while teaching choral music. The lessons I learned from administrators, fellow teachers, staff members, and, especially, students made me a very wealthy man, indeed.

> Dr. Walter Lamble
> Public School Choir Director
> Gone Fishin'

ACKNOWLEDGMENTS

I discovered, in writing this book, that I was not capable of writing everything that needed to be included. In addition to the friends who read a chapter here and there and gave me ideas, there were two groups of musicians who added their two cents' worth to chapter 2 (in the section "Choral Sound and Vocal Production") and the Epilogue.

These, then, are the people who helped me put this together: Jon Carreira, Stirling Culp, Deanna Demes, Brian Farrell, Nancy Goebel, Carl Johnson, John Leman, Judy Moe, Stevie Rawlings, Jan Redick, Myrna Reynolds, Bill Schnell, Mike Schwartzkopf, David Walter, Bill Winnett, and Debbie Wittstein.

I have undoubtedly left some people out, and for that I heartily apologize. "Senior moments," you know.

Thanks also to everyone who didn't laugh when I said I wanted to write a book. I really appreciate everyone who threw me support throughout this project. I hope you enjoy it.

A HANDBOOK FOR
BEGINNING
CHORAL
EDUCATORS

1

GETTING STARTED

A. Building a Choral Program

I sincerely hope that your first job is one that thrusts you into a situation where there is no established program or where the program is on its last (first) legs.

That statement may sound very strange to you. The reason I write this is because if that first contract is in a fancy school with a great program, you are not going to be challenged with the opportunity to create a program that is completely of your doing. You may have to teach three or four years before you really feel ownership of the program. Much better to be in charge from the beginning.

If you do have the enviable experience of being able to create your own program, you will need to address several questions. Probably the most important of these is how to structure the program. Will the goal be to prepare choirs to perform chamber music? Will the choirs explore many different styles? Will the program be centered on the school's show choir? Will you concentrate on jazz or gospel or musical theater?

There is merit in each one of these approaches, but it is my opinion that students must be allowed to have experiences with many styles of music. If a choir sings only "classical" literature, its members are being cheated out of exploring the wealth of choral music that exists outside the classics, including jazz, old standards, pop, and multicultural music. I am aware of a number of programs where the goal of every student in the program is to be chosen to participate in the school's madrigal singers or show choir or . . . Once that happens the student signs up for his or her preferred choir each year. Gone are the daily lessons in sight-singing; gone is the opportunity to learn about French diction. And gone are many other opportunities. The goal and focus of the class is to prepare the next show, to win the next contest, to perfect performance in one specific area. It must be said that some schools have been able to prepare shows, win contests, and still have students performing music of the standard repertoire and sight-singing and acquiring basic skills of musicianship. (A superhuman task, and I wish I could tell you how they do it. If you know a director in your area who has accomplished all of these goals, learn from him or her.)

Our students deserve more. They need to be exposed to the Beethoven "Halleluiah" from *The Mount of Olives,* and they must learn to perform a Kirby Shaw jazz piece in a stylistically appropriate manner, and Morley's "Sing We and Chant It" should be a part of their repertoire. They should experiment with various tone production methods. Where is the tone placed when performing jazz? Is it different for a concert piece? What needs to change to make a gospel song sound authentic? All of these are questions that will never be addressed in a choir which performs only one type of music.

Although I have never tested the following model, it seems to me to be a most logical thing to do in a young program.

First, establish a mixed choir which addresses the needs of many types of singers. Its size will probably be determined by the number of boys initially interested in singing. For my taste, a mix of two thirds SA and one third TB is ideal. The male voice seems to be stronger at the high school level. (Of course there are lots of exceptions to that statement, but I do believe it is true in most cases.)

An aside: You may very well have to "punt" on this one; my first choir was composed of thirty-eight girls and three boys. You do what you have to do to get the program started. Just keep things in perspective. The ratio above is where you are heading, not where you start.

After that group has been set up, there will probably still be a group of girls who want to sing. Logic dictates that an SSA ensemble should be established. These two groups, then, become the backbone of the program. As students become interested in the program, second sections of each of these choruses can be established. At some point in the development of the young program, it might be wise to set up a class just for those boys whose voices have not yet changed. That group needs a lot of psychological strokes as well as musical attention. When these voices are interpolated into a mixed choir, they wreck the sound of the alto section, and they run the very real risk of vocal damage if they are forced to sing tenor.

Although it certainly defies the common practice of "the mixed choir is the 'top' choir," don't be hesitant to group your best females into one ensemble. Consider not creating choirs by proficiency level; use year in school as the only determinant for membership in an ensemble. Try randomly assigning students to groups. Let students choose their own ensemble placement. The options are many; structure the program in the vocally healthiest manner, offering as wide a range of music to each student as possible.

B. Choosing and Purchasing Music

One of the first things you are going to have to do as you start your first school year is order music for the choirs or choose music out of your files. I usually employ five methods of finding music for my groups each year. There are certainly others, but try these for starters.

1. Peruse Samples from Publishers

Over the course of a year, the major publishers send out mass mailings containing recent publications from their houses. You will be inundated with Top 40 and folk chorals, and you will receive a lot of holiday music, much of it too Christian in text for the average public school. Remember, these mailings also go to church choirs. Any standard/classical choral literature will be recent editions. These editions could be invaluable because they simplify a piano part, or because they offer a tenor part with a lower tessitura, or because they reflect recent research findings. Many of these releases, however, are merely clones of existing editions.

Having pointed out all the problems inherent in studying new releases from publishers, I must say that this method of evaluating music for inclusion in your choral library is invaluable because it involves interaction with the publishers themselves. Use it as one method of getting to know the available literature.

2. Look at the Sample Copies Available at the Music Store Where You Purchase Your Music

Many of the copies available at your local music store are the same as those received in the mail from the publishers, but there will be more to see. Music will be there from publishers not represented in the mass mailings, and you will find alternative voicings in much of the music you received. It is worth your time to examine these to find, say, an SAB voice part edition of a pop ballad you liked in SATB. A down year for boys? Look for TTB in place of TTBB. Providing alternative voicings is a very useful service for the music educator in and of itself. The big problem here is that you will see only new arrangements. A lot of show and jazz choir material will be on display, which is terrific for choosing music for those ensembles. On the down side, you will have to look elsewhere for standard choral literature.

3. Do a Thorough Search of the Existing Choral Library at Your School

This could be a very daunting task if it takes place in a school or church that has a well-established choral program. Every piece in that library was deemed worthy by one of your predecessors. Take/ make the time to look at every piece.

AN IMPORTANT NOTE: If it doesn't already exist, start a single-copy file of the entire library's holdings. It is a simple thing to do since you are going through the entire library already. Take one copy of each song you look at, and put it in a folder of its own, and label it with name, voicing, publication information, and location in the library. Start a file drawer for pieces in each voicing: SATB (will need more space than the others), SAB (SSAB), SSA (SSSAAA, etc.), TTBB (TBB, TTB), two-part, and unison. Once this is complete, perusing the library becomes a breeze.

In this process you will discover a lot of good literature and a lot that doesn't meet your needs. You will find "old chestnuts," songs that were very standard at one time and which crop up every so often in choral programs. They never seem to outlive their usefulness. You will discover pieces long out of print that fit your needs to a "t." The only difficulty if this occurs is that it is virtually impossible to get enough copies for your choir if there are not enough copies in the file.

ANOTHER IMPORTANT NOTE: MENC: The National Association for Music Education offers a form which you can send to a publisher to request permission to copy music which is POP, permanently out of print. I have used this form often, and I have never been denied permission. Once I was asked to send a check for 15 cents per copy I made. Using the same form you may request permission to copy music that is TOP, temporarily out of print.

You will also discover the so-called classics of choral literature, the masses, the oratorios, and movements from extended works of all time periods. Depending on the structure of your program, these may form the backbone of your choral repertoire. If they do, try to at least look through original versions of these works before you consider edited, adapted, or arranged versions of the same. Being able to look through these originals is one of the great advantages of having a well-organized and well-cataloged choral library.

Surrounding these discoveries, you will find much standard choral literature from which to pick music for your present students. It will never be a mistake to choose Gene Puerling's arrangement of "Georgia on My Mind" by Hoagy Carmichael, or John Miller's arrangement of "John Henry," or "Cantique de Jean Racine" by Fauré. These are chorales of several genres that will never go out of style. There should be lots of them in a well-stocked choral library.

4. Search Your Personal Library Both for Music and for Memories

Chances are good that you have been involved in choral music for a number of years at a number of levels. There are pieces you have performed that were particularly pleasing to you, that made an impact on you. Find copies of those pieces and peruse them for their appropriateness to your needs. It is probable that a young mixed ensemble will not do Samuel Barber's *Reincarnations*, no matter how much you loved them when you sang them in the graduate chorale.

However, I have often programmed Alice Parker's arrangement of "Hark, I Hear the Harps Eternal" as a result of my having sung it as an undergraduate.

5. Search the Internet

By entering some generic term like "choral music publishers," you will be instantly given entrance to most of the major publishers in business today. If you are interested in the music of a small house, enter that name—e.g., Mark Foster Music—and you will be directed (in this case) to Shawnee Press, which now owns Mark Foster Publications. When you find the publishing house you are seeking, chances are very good that they will have a link to their recent publications. But if you keep looking, you will also find a link to their catalog, which is where you can do some major searching. Depending on the size of the house and their purchase policy, they may let you order online, or they may direct you to use a local distributor.

Whatever you find while online, you will have enjoyed the immediacy that can only be offered on the Internet. You will have lost the individual contact with a retailer, but if you have a good idea what you are looking for, and if you are in a hurry, it is hard to beat using your computer instead of your feet. I'm an old dog, and I am just learning the new tricks offered through technology, but it is a wonderful world of assistance to every teacher.

Having exhausted all four of these options, you probably will have enough music to fill the folders for several years. Now all you need to do is pare it down to one concert's literature. Once you have chosen the literature, you need to order it. Here is a short guide to ordering choral music. There are three normal avenues to follow when ordering. You will learn which one you prefer, but all are perfectly acceptable.

One way to get your music is to *buy through a local music store.* The advantage to this is that you can develop a personal relationship with the owner of the store, and this relationship could lead to big discounts; notification of sales, new literature, etc.; and an understanding creditor when someone in the chain loses a purchase order or provides incorrect information. These can be major gifts to one who works as hard as you do.

Another method is to *buy from an established "jobber."* There are companies who represent multiple (usually all) publishers. Their catalogs are extensive and well organized. The downside is that they tend to push the latest releases on you by offering them in attractive packages with other new releases. Sometimes they go so far as to suggest buying a complete concert in one pre-prepared packet. The upside is that almost every title is available very rapidly because the in-stock holdings are so great. Also, the "off the beaten track" items you want may be more readily available through a jobber. Your personal allegiance to an individual marketer is the missing ingredient when working with a regional corporation rather than a local one.

Buy directly from a publisher. The obvious advantage is that you will get exactly what you ask for each time; the disadvantages are several. You may get lost in the shuffle of a large publishing house, and more important, some publishers will sell only to retailers, not to individual buyers. This option is usually used only when the other two have failed.

Choosing the music for each of your choral organizations is one of the most important decisions you will make. The music needs to be of the highest quality, regardless of style or level, and at the same time it needs to have both audience and singer appeal. It is not an impossible task, but it *is* time consuming. Don't skimp on time; the results will be well worth your investment.

C. Before School Begins

If you are lucky enough to sign a contract in advance of the opening of school, there is much you can do to facilitate your first days in the classroom with students. Depending on the way the school schedule is established, you may be able to have some impact on the structure of your program and the set-up of your school day. The worst-case scenario is that the schedule is written in stone, and student schedules are equally unchangeable. This is what you encounter if you walk into a program that is well established and has been carefully tailored by the previous teacher. In this case, you take what is given to you and hope for some internal flexibility as the school year progresses. The happiest situation you could wish for (if you inherit an established program) is one in which you are presented with a list of names of students interested in choral music and a blank slate as far as the schedule is concerned. If that is the case, you can begin to mold your program from the first day you sign the contract. But it also means a lot of extra work for you.

I have no desire to repeat myself in a book this short, so I would guide you toward the earlier section "Building a Choral Music Program" to help you make decisions about what classes to establish. Instead, let's start with how to people those classes.

If you sat down with your lists and assigned students to classes on the basis of their year in school, sex, and previous experience, you could probably make some intelligent decisions without the need for an audition. However, there is a certain amount of additional information I would collect from each student before making class assignments.

The quickest, although not necessarily the most efficient, way to collect this information is a mailing to the homes of the students. Most schools have a mailing budget to cover situations exactly like this one.

The letter you send should welcome the student to the choral program and introduce you as the new person on the block. Explain that you will soon be setting up the various choirs, and that you would like to get some information from them to help you make the right decisions. Some of the questions I would normally like answered are

What grade are you in? (Maturity of voice quality is tied to age.)
Have you sung in choirs? (Nothing beats experience.)
What other singing have you done? (Solo work, rock bands, family quartets, church groups, and all of the other possible experiences show a level of commitment to singing. And that commitment will be essential for some of the activities of the choral department.)
What is your grade point average or class rank? (A smart person will normally be a smart singer—not necessarily a good singer, but a smart one.)

Do you play an instrument? (An instrumental background, especially a piano background, almost always ensures some level of sight-reading ability.)

If you are a pianist, how may years have you studied? (You will be searching for accompanists.)

Would your parent or guardian be interested in helping out with choral projects? (You are going to need this support when you plan your school year.)

There is a lot more useful information to be gathered, but the letter should be short enough that you stand a reasonable chance of having it returned. On the basis of the answers to this questionnaire I would begin separating the students into at least two groups: a mixed group and a female ensemble. These two groups, even if they are small, can provide the beginnings of a structure to your choral program.

Another way to proceed to make judgments as to choral placement is to audition the students. Although the return will be lower than the return on a questionnaire, you should send out a letter introducing yourself and inviting them to sing for you over the summer. If there is summer secretarial help available, enlist one or more of the secretaries to call each student and invite him or her to audition. (For your sake, it is probably best for you to establish a week for these auditions.) If you decide on this route, you should be aware from the outset that many of the students will be frightened to sing for you, and they won't sign up for an audition of their own volition. Some students will be too reticent to sing in private. They may remove their names from the list rather than submit to an audition. Keep a list of those people; they can often be cajoled into joining choir in spite of an audition once they see the department functioning.

If you decide on the audition option, here is how I'd proceed:

As with the questionnaire, collect pertinent logistic information.

List previous singing experiences. (This will show relative scope of activity and give you an idea of their involvement in music.)

I wouldn't ask much more than that on the audition sheet. Keep the rest of the questions for the audition.

Here is how I would proceed with any first-time audition:

1. Sing through a couple of common songs with the student until you sense they are beginning to be at ease singing for you. It is a great help if you can accompany yourself and the student to add even more strength to the support you are lending the young singer.
2. Vocalize to establish approximate vocal range. Although it is not an optimal situation, sing with the student who is too nervous to do a good job alone. Do not comment on anything other than range at this point.
3. Sight-sing a simple four-bar phrase. Allow the student to back out of this portion of the audition. To one who cannot sight-sing, being forced to endure a sight-singing audition is sheer agony.
4. Sing a song. It may be something of their own choosing. When they choose to audition with their own song you will probably have to provide accompaniment.

On the basis of what you hear in these four categories you should be able to make initial placements into the choirs you have set up. You can continue to audition once the school year has begun for as long as the counseling staff permits drops and adds.

There are several things you must be aware of as you audition these students.

Don't be fooled into thinking that the highest voices are the sopranos and the tenors and the lowest voices the altos and basses. Especially with the women, the presence of a strong "chest" voice can fool the teacher into assuming a girl is an alto. The best gauge we have in determining altos from sopranos is where the break occurs between head voice and chest voice. These terms are not universal, but, briefly, chest voice is the low, gutsy voice at the bottom end of the girl's range. It is the voice that young children usually use when they sing. Head voice is that sound in the upper part of the range which is often more light and delicate than the chest sound. Young singers sometimes drag their feet when urged to sing in head voice because it sounds thin and weak to them. It will remain that way until it is developed.

In an audition there are two different ways to evaluate the voice of a girl. The first is to vocalize her upward from a very low pitch. As she ascends the scale, one of several things will happen. She may flip over into a head tone with no discernible difference in the sound. That student can sing either part; put her in the section that the quality of her voice best fits. If the sound is rich and warm, let her sing alto; if there is a light quality to the sound, soprano is probably the choice for her. It is possible (and possibly safer) to get the same information by vocalizing downward from a very high pitch. Again, listen for the change from head voice to chest voice. It may be a bit elusive; that is why I prefer vocalizing upwards.

Sometimes a girl will vocalize up and the sound will get more and more forced-sounding, and all of a sudden she will quit, saying that she can't sing any higher. What she is telling you is that no one has ever helped her develop her head voice, and all she knows how to work with is her chest voice. At this point you have no choice but to assign her to the alto part, but she will need constant supervision to make sure she is not pushing that voice too high in her range. When you work with her privately, vocalize her downward, beginning on a tone high enough that she has no choice but to use head voice. Insist that she stay in head voice as long as possible as she descends through her break into chest voice. As she learns to cover that break, the high voice will become stronger, and she will be able to help you on the soprano part occasionally.

Finally, the young woman may vocalize far too high in the chest voice; her sound will become very harsh and "belted." There are a lot of models for this sound: Broadway, recordings, and bands are three good examples. To get this young singer to agree with you that this is not her true sound, and that she must develop her head sound so that it is as strong as her chest, requires a trust in you that you have not yet earned. Let her sing both parts on alternate numbers. Give her lots of encouragement until she is ready to work with you on developing the whole range.

Typing young men's voices is a similar process, but much simpler. If a boy sounds like a bass, and he can sing in the bass range, let him sing bass. As he does more and more singing, his range will begin to grow. At that point the two of you can find some tenor things for him and he can experiment.

Two different types of voice will fall into the tenor range. The first is the young man who really is or will grow to be a tenor. His quality is probably lighter than his bass counterparts; he can generally sing higher, and he has a natural transition into his high voice, his falsetto. The other group of high school–aged men who should be assigned to tenor are those whose voices have not changed or are in the process of changing. Although some may disagree, I do believe that if these young voices will be assigned to a mixed chorus, they must be treated as men, not women. It is true that you will have to rewrite every song to fit their ranges; you must not force an unchanged voice to sing tones that are not in its range. I much prefer that to assigning a young man to the alto section. Life is hard enough on those guys who mature late.

A word about the previously mentioned falsetto voice. Falsetto is that remnant of the boy voice that is left at the top of a man's range. It is absolutely essential that young male singers learn to use falsetto to protect their voices. A good exercise for developing the falsetto range while helping it blend into the mid-voice is to pick a pitch at the very top of the range and sing it on an *oo* or *ee* vowel. Once the pitch is established, slide very slowly down to the lowest sound in the voice, work on staying in falsetto as long as possible. (If any of the boys can't find their falsetto voice, say to them, "The Lion Sleeps Tonight." With the image of that song in mind, it is usually much easier for them to find the sound. If any still can't find that upper range, consider the possibility of some kind of vocal damage, usually temporary, from over-enthusiasm at last week's football game.)

You will read this often in these pages: never harm a young voice. Assigning students to the best voice parts for them is a very positive step toward protecting the voices in your choirs.

A related note: Don't assume that the highest and lowest voices are the "best" voices. As you build your choirs, certainly be aware of what student can "ping" out the high B-flats and the low E-flats, but a lot of good sopranos may not be able to comfortably sing above a G when you first encounter them. If the sound is good, make adding the range one of your projects for the year.

After you have a rough idea what your curriculum will look like, get a yearly performance schedule drawn up and on the school calendar, even before you see the students for the first time. You can always change it if it looks like things won't be prepared, but an early establishment of the performing calendar accomplishes three things:

1. When a date is on the school calendar, it is usually kept rather sacred by other activities in the building. The fewer conflicts you run into with other activities, the better your presentations will be and the healthier your relationship with the rest of the school will be.
2. Students will know you mean business when you tell them their attendance at concerts and other activities is required. You will be amazed at how many excuses students (and their parents) will manufacture to get the evening off.
3. Parents will also understand that you are serious about concert attendance. In my last job, we used our concerts (one per quarter) as the students' final grade for the quarter. When parents understand that the A in Choir is as useful to the GPA as the one in AP English, it is amazing how few students miss concerts. If this is a new policy, you will hear a lot of "You can't do that" and "That's not fair." But if your counseling staff is supportive, everyone will soon realize that, indeed, you can do it.

To achieve this final result, I suggest preparing a schedule of required concerts for the entire year to hand out to the students shortly after school has begun. About a week later, I would send a copy of the schedule home, along with costume requirements, time commitments, and other concert requirements. I would ask each family to review the entire sheet and return an agreement that states their child will be at all concerts. This letter is also useful for requesting adult help in supervising the concert.

A final duty that can be done before the school year begins to make your opening go more smoothly is to prepare folders and rehearsal material for the first couple of weeks. Make sure each student assigned to your classes has a folder containing sight-singing material, warm-ups, and several choral pieces to begin with. If the pieces need to be changed three weeks into the quarter to accommodate a group that is more or less advanced than you originally thought, that's fine. You will save a lot of time if you have prepared material for each student in advance.

Some sample forms and letters can be found in Appendix A. As you look at these, be aware that all of these can be easily recreated and saved using word-processing or desktop publishing software. I suggest you use the computer any time you can.

Getting Started: Exercises

1. You have just accepted a job at H. G. Wells High School. There has been no outstanding choral tradition at Wells, and the initial enrollment for choir is thirty-two girls and four boys. All the boys are freshmen. How would you set up a program for these students, and what would you do in your first rehearsal?
2. You signed a contract in May for a job teaching at Mozart Tech High School. Included in your musical day are three periods of chorus. You have twenty-three boys and sixty-one girls. They are divided more or less evenly among the three grades present at MTHS. Show how you would use these three periods to provide the best choral experience for each of these students.
3. One of the choirs you will teach in the fall is a girls' chorus composed of forty girls, mostly seniors. Design their first concert of about a half hour. This is a mostly serious concert. Use at least two of the methods discussed in the chapter for reviewing music: working on the Internet, reviewing a choral library, checking out new publications from a publisher, looking at the music at a local music store, or using your own personal library. Provide title, publisher, octavo number, and cost for each piece.
4. Same assignment as above, but design a pops concert for an SATB group of relatively young voices.
5. You've signed a contract for your first job. It looks as if your

numbers will support a small mixed chorus and a mid-sized girls' chorus. Dusty, a sophomore girl, has come in for an audition. Using the audition sheet in Appendix A, describe in detail her audition, and finally, make a recommendation for her choral placement. Don't forget that parents want reasons for decisions.

6. Rusty is Dusty's younger brother. He is an incoming freshman who just loves to sing; his ability level is yours to find out. Same process as in number 5.

2

CHORAL BASICS IN THE REHEARSAL

A. Warming Up the Choir

Most of us have begun almost every choral rehearsal with a series of vocalizations and tongue twisters. We perform these without question, realizing that it is essential to "warm up" before we begin to rehearse. Our directors have often told us that just as an athlete must stretch his or her muscles before engaging in any strenuous activity, so a singer must get the vocal muscles in shape before making music. There is no question that this is a useful analogy and one which explains the warm-up period to the singer.

From the conductor's standpoint, however, it is not enough for the warm-up period to merely get the vocal muscles in shape before making music. Each exercise should be chosen to accomplish a specific task; warm-ups should be planned by the conductor before the rehearsal begins. It is not enough to just "la-la" for a few minutes before beginning the "real rehearsal."

Certainly one of these tasks is to get the muscles in shape. Depending on the time of day and the amount of talking and singing the choristers have indulged in, this part of the warm-up period takes on different complexions. Assuming that the rehearsal is scheduled during a typical school day, the warm-ups should begin in a fairly relaxed manner. Good old-fashioned vocalizing on pure vowels in limited ranges is in order. These are well-known exercises and need very little discussion. Five-note scales which rise from a comfortable mid-range point to gradually addressing the upper ranges are useful. Descending scales that slowly accommodate the lower range are also appropriate. One important thing to remember is the difference in the various voice types in the choir. To warm up the upper range for the sopranos will cause the lower female voices to strain unnecessarily. The same is true for the higher and lower male voices. If the warm-ups for the day are intended to include these upper ranges, individual voice types should be vocalized separately. It is similarly important in all warm-ups (and in all singing) that the lower ranges for all singers not be pushed.

Crisp diction may be one of the goals for the day's rehearsal. This is where the tongue twisters come into play. "Red leather, yellow leather," and all the other consonant-laden exercises we have learned are excellent to accomplish this task. In addition to bringing the singers' attention to the necessity of clean articulation of these consonants, these exercises can be a lot of fun for the singer. A simple but energetic accompaniment at the keyboard can make this part of the warm-up period bright. While these exercises should be an extension of the range-developing warm-ups, it is again important not to overextend the voice in terms of range.

To plan in advance of the rehearsal how long this part of the warm-up period should last is usually not possible. Of course a plan of action must exist, but each day will dictate the amount of vocal warm-up necessary for the choir to move on to the next phase of rehearsal. The weather outside the building has an effect on how much warm-up time is necessary, as does the weather inside the building.

An aside: Expect to work around the heating and cooling system in your building. More often than not, your room will be too hot or too cold for some of the students. Keep a sweater or flannel shirt handy for yourself, and encourage students to make similar accommodations. It is easier and more productive than constantly complaining.

In addition to serving the function of getting the vocal mechanism ready for rehearsal, warm-ups should prepare singers for the specific music to be practiced during the period. If one of the song excerpts to be rehearsed is an a cappella unison section, special attention should be paid to vowel formations and careful listening. Perhaps forming the choir into a circle so they can sing inwards to each other is in order. If an energetic, highly rhythmic piece is on the docket, exercises which stress rhythm should be used. Adding physicality to the warm-ups (bouncing, snapping, clapping, whatever works for you) is helpful. Don't limit movement during warmups to highly rhythmic activities. Swaying, conducting, tracing phrases, and marking the direction of musical line are all useful to the singer. If you are planning to rehearse Bach, it would be wise to include some of the German vowel and consonant sounds in your routine, and if Fauré is planned, time would be well spent on preparing the vowels that are unique to the French language.

Basically, the thing to remember about the warm-up period is not to let it become a mindless period of time that must be endured before rehearsing the printed score. Relate it to the day and to its vocal demands. Prepare the voice for the next portion of the rehearsal. There is a motto in the field of medicine that says something to the effect of "above all, do no harm." The same applies to the choral director; the worst thing we can do is to harm a voice. Never allow a singer to push or strain the voice. No song is worth it; no role is worth it. Healthy warming up can be the key to this vocal safety.

See Appendix B for some exercises that can be useful.

B. The Unison Sound

Producing a unison sound in the choir may very well be one of the most difficult chores a director can undertake. That unison is definitely one of the most thrilling sounds a choir can produce. Some directors—young and experienced alike—make the mistake of assuming that because there is only one part to learn a piece is simple to perform. They likewise assume that the piece or section of the piece that is unison will not have the impact of a big eight-part texture. They are wrong on both counts.

"What wondrous love is this, oh my soul, oh my soul? What wondrous love is this . . ." Those of us who have been in the business for a while will instantly recognize these words, and many will have performed that beautiful Christiansen arrangement. Because of its accessibility of notes, choirs of all ages and ability levels have performed it. But it was not until I heard the St. Olaf Choir perform it that I fully realized the brilliance of that unison choral presentation. Each sound was a gem, molded to perfection and creating a line of beauty and intensity as is seldom heard. This simple unison line was able to produce almost life-changing results in a listener.

A note: Throughout this handbook you will find that I refer to specific pieces of music. These are all standards in the high school choral repertoire. Don't let any of them get past you; learning them is worth your time.

To achieve a fine unison sound, the choir must perform a number of musical elements in a unison manner. First—and this is the one goal almost everyone strives to achieve—everyone in the choir must be singing the same notes. Very few of us go wrong here. Hopefully we have taught our choirs to sight-read music so that singing the right note is a given. If we are still caught in the land of rote learning, we still usually learn the right notes.

Closely tied to singing the same notes is singing them in tune, singing a unison *pitch*. If soprano #1 is singing a pitch dead on, while soprano #2 is a little bit sharp and soprano #3 a little bit flat, there is no possibility of a unison pitch, which is one of the aspects of a unison sound. Making sure the choir sings in tune is a constant area of concern. Singers must listen carefully to themselves, but also to all those around them. It only takes one out-of-tune singer to ruin the sound of a section, thus adversely affecting the unison sound we are seeking.

A third area for attention is unison *vowel* production. As has been mentioned before, vowel sounds are the lifeblood of a choral text. It is absolutely essential that all singers use the exact same vowels when articulating a piece. If all the tenors in the section sing a warm, rounded *ah* vowel on the first word of that "Wondrous Love," but one man sings a very bright vowel with a wide side-to-side mouth opening, there is no chance the section will produce a unison sound. Again, the onus of that vowel production is on the singer. Listening is the key. The conductor shares responsibility for correcting any problems that he or she hears. It will probably be necessary to zero in on any offender and make him or her aware of the problem.

A word about singling out one chorister for criticism: Make sure you know your choir well enough that you know how each member would react if criticized on an individual basis. It is true that group critiques are basically useless, but you must never neglect the singers' feelings. It may be necessary to be inventive in correcting the problem.

Probably the easiest of the major components of a unison sound to produce is unison *dynamics*. Even though it seems like that statement should be obvious and universally acknowledged, every choir has balance problems of one sort or another. Perhaps the alto section is dominated by one voice; perhaps the bass section has two singers who are conspicuously shy when it comes to producing enough sound. Whatever the problem, all choirs experience balance problems within and between sections.

As is true of the other components of a unison sound, good dynamic balance between sections is a product of careful listening on the parts of both the director and the choir. There are a couple of tricks which come to mind that have proven effective for me in improving dynamic balance between sections. Seat the choir in quartets; that often helps the young singers hear other voice types more easily, and that helps them balance volume more accurately. Another strategy is to seat the singers in a circle so that they are singing in to each other. If your rehearsal space allows for that kind of set-up, try it; it may prove to be very effective.

The responsibility for holding back the exuberant singer and encouraging the reticent one lies mainly with the choral director. He or she can control this situation by identifying the students who are causing difficulties of balance within the sections and giving them positive notes on how to go about correcting the problem. Obviously the most important solution is to listen more carefully. Move the soft singer to a spot between two confident singers; direct him or her to increase dynamics until he feels that the sounds are about equal. Do just the opposite with the too-loud singer. Have that choir member balance the sound between him or her and two fairly quiet singers.

Other useful activities involve vocalizations that are created for dynamic practice. One example: Sing a pitch on an *ah* vowel, moving from *pp* to *ff* and back to *pp*. Move up a half step and repeat. An exercise which challenges the mind at the same time as practicing dynamics is this: Direct the choir to sing a given pitch at a volume level you determine. Call out an interval and a new dynamic: "up a perfect fourth, *mezzoforte*." Once all choir members have agreed on the new pitch and the new dynamic, repeat; and so on.

There are certainly other things a choir must do to achieve an effective unison sound (create unison articulation and style, for instance), but these four — *notes, intonation, vowels, and dynamics* — are the main areas to be addressed. When unison exists in each of these areas, a sound will be produced by the choir that thrills the ears of listener and singer alike.

C. Vowels, Diphthongs, and Consonants

1. Vowels

As I work with my own choirs, and as I listen to others, I am aware that the most prevalent, and most easily corrected, problem is that of vowel formations. Standard vocal practice is to achieve a neutral set of vowels that reflect no regional mannerisms. They should capture the correct pronunciation of the language being performed.

There are two main systems for recording on paper the various sounds of the languages we speak and in which we sing. The one which is most accessible but the least precise, especially for languages other than English, is one in which the various vowel sounds are spelled as they are heard. For instance, the pronunciation of the first vowel sound in the word *father* is *ah*. The vowel sound in the word *hot* is also *ah*. It is the sound that is spelled, not the vowel itself. *Who* contains the vowel *oo* and the consonant sound *h*. This system works well for English and Latin, but it has limitations in German, French and most other languages. The system which works equally well in English and in most foreign languages is one which uses the International Phonetic Alphabet. Using the IPA, a student learns a specific symbol for each spoken sound and its variations. Most of the symbols for consonants are the same as their English counterparts. For the remainder of this chapter, all sounds will be spelled in English.

The vowel sounds necessary to perform most, if not all, sounds used in singing English can be formed using two basic mouth positions. The *ah* position allows for the formation of the *ah, oh, oo,* and some humming sounds. To achieve this mouth position, simply drop the jaw as far as it will go without straining; let the tongue lie in the bottom of the mouth with its tip forward, even to touching the lower front teeth. By imitating a yawn or the sensation of sipping water from a fountain, raise the soft palate; the same imagery will allow the throat to open. With the lips in a mostly open position, the *ah* vowel can be produced. A slight closing of the jaw causes the *aw* vowel sound to be produced, and a rounding of the lips will enable the singer to sing an *oh* vowel; a further closing of the jaw and even more rounding of the lips will produce the *oo* vowel, and a final closure of the lips (with the jaws still open) will create a very open hum. The several types of humming will be discussed as they arise.

The second major mouth position is the *ee* position. The *å* (as in *cat*), *eh, ih,* and *ee* vowel sounds are produced in the same way as described above. Let the tongue arch a bit (not too much or the throat may become obstructed). It should lie forward in the mouth; drop the soft palate somewhat from where it was in the *ah* formation; and keep the throat open. Lip positions vary more in this mouth position. To produce the *å* sound, use an *ah* mouth formation, while raising the tongue a little. Careful practice and listening allows the singer to produce an open, clear vowel. It is free from the characteristic flat vowel sound prevalent in some regional areas, while avoiding the open *ah* a sound which sounds so affected when coupled with American English pronunciation.

A slight closing of both the lips and the jaws will allow the singer to produce an *eh* vowel, and closing the lips and jaw another degree will make the *ih* vowel possible. Closing the jaw more creates the *ee* vowel sound. Many choral directors prefer to produce the *ee* sound using this mouth position in combination with an *oo* lip formation to allow for a rounded sound. Some directors tell students to bring in the corners of their mouths to achieve this rounded sound. Using the *ah* lip position tends to spread, causing an overly bright sound.

It is important for the singer and conductor to practice these sounds as a continuum within each of the mouth positions. In other words, a unified sound is produced from vowel sound to vowel sound within a given position: *ah, aw, oh, oo,* and hums are produced with the same basic formation of the mouth; therefore, they share the same vocal quality, even though they exhibit different vowel qualities. The same is true of the vowel sounds produced in the *ee* mouth position.

Every word in the English language can be sung using these sounds or gradations or combinations of them. I have not yet encountered any exceptions.

2. Diphthongs

The combining of two of the pure vowel sounds makes it possible to sing some of the most important sounds in the English language. The result of this combining of sounds is called a diphthong. The vowel sound that is sung for the longer amount of time is called the *primary* sound, and the shorter of the two is called the *vanished* or *secondary* sound. In most cases, the primary vowel is first, while the vanished vowel is added at the end of the diphthong, but there are exceptions.

The long *a* sound is produced using a primary *eh* vowel and a vanished *ee* or *ih* sound; for example,

meh . . . *eek* will produce the word *make;*
heh . . . *eet* produces the word *hate;*
bleh . . . *eem* gives us the word *blame.*

Substituting an *ih* vowel for the vanished *ee* vowel will produce a softer finish to the word, which is the preferred sound for many choral directors and voice coaches.

Combining the *ah* vowel (primary) and the *oo* vowel (secondary) allows the singer to sing the *ow* vowel sound, as in *how.* Examples:

mah . . . *oontun* creates the word *mountain;*
lah . . . *ood* is the way to pronounce *loud.*

Similar to the *ee/ih* substitution, an *oh* vowel may be the preferred secondary vowel sound when singing an *ow* diphthong.

Other often-used diphthongs are the long *i* sound, which is produced using a primary *ah* a vowel in combination with a vanished *ee* or *ih* (*ah* . . . *ee* = *eye*). The most common "backwards" diphthong, the long *u* sound, is the result of combing a vanished *ee* or *ih* vowel sound with a primary *oo* sound; e.g., *few* (*fee* . . . *oo*).

A diphthong is notated by using a full-sized symbol for the primary vowel, and a superscript symbol for the vanished vowel. So, *ah* . . . *ee* (*eye*) is the same as a^i. *Hah* . . . *oo* (*how*) equals ha^u.

A quick review: The sounds produced using the approaches described above are listed here.

ah as in	*father*
aw as in	*caught*
oh as in	*home*
oo as in	*who*
uh as in	*hut*
â as in	*and*
eh as in	*pet*
ih as in	*give*
ee as in	*seek*
ow as in	*how*
a as in	*say*
i as in	*my*
u as in	*few*

In the years during which Fred Waring and his Pennsylvanians were influential in certain areas of choral music, he developed a system for notating the vowel sounds which create the words of a song. This system is very similar to the system described above, and it is published in a pamphlet entitled "Tone Syllables," which is still a part of the Shawnee Press catalog.

3. Consonants

Vowels provide music with sounds which can be sustained for singing. That is their role. Consonants provide the vehicle to separate those sounds into intelligible syllables and words. Most consonants fall very roughly into two categories: voiced and non-voiced. These terms must be fairly self-explanatory, even to the person encountering them in this context for the first time. When producing a voiced consonant, the singer makes a musical sound which exhibits a specific pitch. On the other hand, a non-voiced consonant is a sound that has absolutely no pitch in it and involves no vibration of the vocal folds.

Be aware that the IPA symbol for most consonants is the same as their English counterpart. Some voiced consonants are as follows:

g as in   *mirage*
l as in   *love*
m as in   *more*
n as in   *tune*
ng as in   *sing*
r as in   *rage**
th as in   *than*
v as in   *vote*
z as in   *haze*
zh as in   *azure*

Some non-voiced consonants are as follows:

k as in   *cat*
ch as in   *church*
s as in   *dice*
g as in   *rage**
h as in   *hot* (*h* is technically described as an aspirant)
j as in   *join*
p as in   *perfect*
ph as in   *photo*
qu as in   *queen*
s as in   *safe* (*s* is technically described as a sibilant)
t as in   *take*
th as in   *thin*
x as in   *exchange*

*Some directors choose to roll or tick the *r* at all times, making it a non-voiced consonant on all occasions.

There are several consonants that defy inclusion in either category because, in fact, they contain elements of both. These are the so-called sub-labials. They are made up of a voiced preface to the sound, and then a non-voiced explosion. For example:

b as in   *boy*
d as in   *dawn*
g as in   *God*

That explosion at the end of many consonants is a non-voiced sound. It is very important to the creation of words. When the explosion is left off or understated, especially when the consonant is at the end of a particular word, the word is often unintelligible. Try pronouncing the word *out* without the small puff of air that follows the partial closing of the lips. The sound produced is an unfinished syllable, not unlike a stifled consonant. By the same token, it is important not to overemphasize this final motion or the consonant will take on a stature to the listener that it may not deserve.

An aside from a friend who spent a number of years studying choral techniques with Fred Waring: "Mr. Waring loved *r*'s! Any time a singer could "voice" a consonant sound it became potential for beauty. . . . The plosive *t* sound drove him crazy because it interrupted the sound. It was not dialogue but affected diction, and it made him angry to hear inappropriate popped consonant sounds. In a love song, he wanted English sung as if it were being spoken, not recited." Following this conductor's lead, don't become a slave to any system of pronunciation. Adjust diction to your own ear.

Please remember that the main reasons for using any system of identifying vowel and consonant sounds are to prepare the score for singers who will follow them in the preparation of the work, and to remind oneself of proper pronunciation.

D. Choral Sound and Vocal Production

When I reached the topic of choral sound and vocal production I realized that although I had built most of my teaching around these two concepts, I had trouble putting my thoughts into words. So I contacted a group of my friends and asked them to give me input by answering a few questions relating to that topic. Following are excerpts from their responses. Note that for some of these questions there is general agreement, and for some of the others there is a wide variation in answers. Feel free to agree or disagree with anything you read. The respondents are all outstanding musicians. None of their answers are wrong. Read them all; digest them; put them to the litmus test of your own training and background. Then make up your own mind as to how the questions should be answered.

Question: Please describe the tone quality you feel is appropriate for a high school choir to produce.

Respondent 1: I've heard a wide variety of tone in high school choirs, and have always compared such groups to my personal experience. The appropriate sound should be determined by the students' level of vocal maturity. The sound can be big and hearty or small and pointed. Or, ideally, a combination of sounds/tonal qualities, to express different types of music or even different ideas within the same piece.

Respondent 2: The choral tone quality at the high school level must be based on sound and healthy vocal practices. These singers CAN sing with "cleanliness," intonation, matched vowels, etc. — AND moderated mature tone that is not pushed back into the throat.

Respondent 3: In all cases, vocal production should sound natural, have good resonance and breath support, and not be contrived unless a particular effect is required. Tone which is appropriate to the piece is paramount.

Respondent 4: So many conductors underestimate the capabilities of the teenaged voice; I think that many take the "hands-off" approach and their choirs end up sounding bright and childlike. . . . Ick. I always work toward a more mature sound with depth of tone . . . but it's pretty horrible when that is taken to extremes.

Respondent 5: Open and free, natural and easy, supported and energized, flowing, focused and directed, more vertically than laterally.

Respondent 6: High school students are capable of producing an incredible variety of sounds. Contributing to this variety are some obvious factors of age, ethnic background, selected models imitated consciously or subconsciously, and personal choices. A vocally healthy sound requires the proper coordination of the involved muscles, correct breathing, and minimizing muscular tension. This will enable the singer to produce a wide variety of colors required for the many different types of composition.

Respondent 7: Open, rounded vowels.

Respondent 8: Joyful, light, moving, sensitive, colorful, warm, round.

Respondent 9: To answer this question, you have to consider the repertoire. Tone quality is appropriate to repertoire more than to age groups.

Respondent 10: A good choral sound is well blended, sung with dynamic color and variety.

Respondent 11: There is no one "appropriate" choral sound. I believe that sound will depend on the qualities of the individual voices, and that will change from year to year, from choir to choir. But there are most definitely characteristics which are present in all good choral sounds. The sound must be free from tension and relaxed. Vowels must be unified. Tone must be resonant, and tone must be placed so that it is neither "edgy" or too "dark." Within these parameters a conductor can go about building his choir's appropriate sound.

Question: What is an inappropriate sound for a high school choir?

Respondent 1: Neither an over-produced heavy sound nor a pure "white" sound would be appropriate—as neither is appropriate for the individual singers in the choirs. I must say that I've seen as much vocal damage done from the straight-tone hooty choral tone as from the pushed, over-produced sound.

Respondent 2: In an attempt to produce a more mature sound, high school singers may force their larynx to a very low position.

The resultant sound is inappropriate, as is the sound resulting from a larynx placed too high. A breathy and/or unfocused sound may also be inappropriate. Imitating the vocal production of some pop/ rock stars can be devastating.

Respondent 3: Tense, exaggerated, lowered larynx.

Respondent 4: Cold, heavy, forced, dark, cramped, painful, flat.

Respondent 5: I believe this question depends on style.

Respondent 6:

1. Any sound that is forced;
2. Women singing too high in chest voice;
3. Men screaming in their high range with no knowledge of how to blend into head voice;
4. The opposite of #3—a sound that lacks energy, is breathy and flabby;
5. A sound that is terribly restrained and a vibrato that is unnaturally removed (both are harmful to the voice).

Question: How do or would you go about getting the sound you want?

Respondent 1: I use breathing exercises as warm-ups, always connecting the voice to the breath.

Respondent 2: Working on uniformity of vowels is a big element in choral sound.

Respondent 3: How to get the sound I want from my choir? Practice good basic inhalation and exhalation; practice singing with an open throat; practice consistent vowel formation. Spend time working toward using all resonators. When I taught high school, I always approached tone from the standpoint of diction and breathing . . . and I still do!

Respondent 4: I work the men in their falsetto for about five minutes each day. This tends to make them sing more comfortably in their upper range; they sing with less tension.

Respondent 5: First teach your students the fundamental ideas of vocal technique so that they can sing freely and let their natural emotions be carried on the breath stream. If they are enjoying themselves, they will get it.

Respondent 6: I try every day to find that magic combination of perfect vowel matching, vertical alignment of attacks, and total discipline of turning the diphthong TOGETHER for maximum clarity of text and unification of sound.

Respondent 7:

A. Design a conducting gesture appropriate for the desired sound.

B. Demonstrate with a recording, your voice, or another singer's voice.

C. Describe the sound you want.

Respondent 8: The warm-up period at the beginning of the rehearsal is a time to work on choral sound. During that time it is possible to work on quality of sound, breath support, shaping of phrases, resonance, shaping of vowels, articulation, and dynamic levels, among others.

Respondent 9: Warm-ups are very important, both for individuals and for the group. Individually I hope the students will come to rehearsal having made some sounds, if only enough to have their voices awake. As a group we work on vowel formation, tone quality, and blending from one register to another more than anything else.

Question: What are common problems associated with placement of tone, and what can you do to correct them?

Respondent 1: Are they all keeping the backs of their mouths open inside (the tonsil area), while allowing the sound to resonate naturally against the front of their faces? And again, are they all singing with uniform vowel sounds, which can help place the sound, keep it from being too far back (woofy) or too far forward (shrill, thin)?

Respondent 2: Young singers tend to place the tone either too far in the face/head (making bright tone), or based too deep in the throat, causing it to be too heavy and throaty.

Respondent 3: I have the students imitate various types of singing: opera, an Italian street singer, Gomer Pyle (both sounds), Frank Sinatra, Barbra Streisand, a little child, a lullaby. Then we talk about placement as they used it in these various types of singing.

Respondent 4: Proper placement should be a result of correct singing rather than a conscious attempt to aim one's sound at a desired area.

Respondent 5: Placement in the mask and sending the notes out on a well-supported airstream are what make for beautiful singing.

Respondent 6: One of the successful techniques I use to give my students a sense of proper placement of tone is to ask them to imitate various sounds which are familiar to them: an "opera" singer, a "jazz" singer, an "ever-the-hiss-church-choir" alto. We then discuss and practice the ways in which these sounds were produced.

Respondent 7: Warming up with an exercise that rehearses changing a sound from very throaty to very bright is very effective in finding an appropriate placement for the daily rehearsal. I look for that point on the "placement continuum" that is suitable for the work to be done. For example, I would choose a brighter, more frontal placement for a musical theater rehearsal than I would for a concert rehearsal. I always work close to the middle of that continuum; that is a safe area for the voice and an effective area for quality of tone.

Respondent 8: Do you know the book *In Quest of Answers: Interviews with American Choral Conductors*? It's edited by Carole Glenn and published by Hinshaw. Carole asked roughly thirty conductors their opinions regarding all sorts of subjects . . . and one question was "Do you have a preference in terms of tone quality?" The answers are fascinating. . . . The large majority say that they "preach" a basic healthy tone quality which then can be adapted to any historical period.

Respondent 9: As you know, straight tone is seemingly becoming a preference in choral culture (in some geographical areas at some age levels) today due to the influence of the English choirs, the Scandinavian choirs, some of the new Eastern European works that are being discovered, and the neo-romantic thick chord writing that is so prevalent in twenty-first-century choral composition. It also works well for jazz. Unfortunately, I find this sound tremendously uninteresting—as if the beauty of the vocalism is being subjugated to the "beauty" of the composition. . . . I kind of always thought they should work together.

Respondent 10: If a good vocal tone is the "top of the mountain" of choral music, I believe there is no one way, but many ways, of achieving it.

Respondent 11: The comments that I've made apply to a classical choir, not a show choir. I believe that other rules come in to play when dealing with show choirs. An example of this would be that women may use some chest sounds when singing contemporary music, and vowels are certainly more spread for both the men and women.

Respondent 12: At the high school level, artistic dividends usually come from the choirs that have been allowed to experience a wide variety of sounds. Warm-up periods are an excellent time to experience these varieties.

Question: Discuss vocal production.

Respondent 1: Basic Components:
1. "Check Points" of Good Posture
   a. Weight well balanced over the balls of both feet
   b. Knees and hips relaxed and flexible (like when skiing or skating!)
   c. Abdominal and lower back muscles open and uncramped
   d. Shoulders stretched wide and chest/rib cage open
   e. Head sits straight, and face, forehead, chin are relaxed (no wrinkles on young faces!)
2. Breathing exercises and technique built on letting the diaphragm function naturally. Correct breathing goes "low"— the abdominal muscles are relaxed so that the diaphragm sinks freely when inhaling (rib muscles and abdomen are distended after a deep breath). The trick in singing is then learning to expel the breath slowly and steadily. When we sing a song, we sing a group of notes on one breath. The notes generally carry a group of words which convey a thought. If we break up the phrase by breathing in the middle, it spoils the flow of the melody and the meaning of the words. The airstream is controlled by the diaphragm and the muscles of the rib cage and lower abdomen. These

muscles slowly and gradually exert pressure inwards which supports the air pressure in the lungs. This air passes up and out through the throat, which contains the vocal chords. The breath pressure sets the vocal chords in vibration. (It is important that good posture is practiced here, so that the chest never sinks down and allows the breathing system to collapse. In good singing, the tone is always supported by controlled breath).

3. Vocal Resonance. A good singer imagines or "hears" the sound he wants to make before he sings it. He knows how high or low the tone is, the placement, the dynamics, the color and character of the words he wants to sing. This is important in preparing a phrase. For example, the higher we sing, the more room we need to make in our mouths by dropping the jaw.

4. Diction. Without the clear pronunciation of consonants and vowels, even the loveliest singing misses its mark. It is important for young singers to work on exercises which show them where to place the pure vowels and then how to add the lip, tip-of-the-tongue, and back-of-the-tongue consonants.

5. Enjoyment. Singing should be a healthy mixture of intelligent thinking, physical control, and joy! Without the elements of heart and soul, singing is just notes and doesn't communicate.

Respondent 2: Good vocal production? Keep your larynx down and your diaphragm down, and you're halfway there! How's that? Something that has always worked for me is my voice teacher's idea of "that old Italian cry" just below the waistline.

Respondent 3: Each singer produces a unique sound determined, in part, by his or her genetic make-up and the muscular/skeletal configuration inherited from the parents. An interesting feature of the human voice is that the muscular flexibility allows for the production of a wide array of sounds. Therefore, individual tone production, in most cases, will be determined by the wishes of the individual and/or by the suggestions of the individual's vocal coach.

Respondent 4: I realize that my answer to a question about tone production is going to suffer when compared to those of the other panelists, who have seriously studied voice most of their lives. The way I go about singing and producing the sound I want is to just do it. I read the text of what I am singing very carefully and then I open my mouth and try to create a tone that expresses those words. I suppose I manipulate my tongue and my lips and my diaphragm and all that, but I am unaware of it. I hunt for a quality that expresses the lyric. The production of vocal sound is achieved by a movement of air emanating in the lungs, supported by the diaphragm, freely passing over the activated vocal folds, and resonated in the throat, mouth, and nasal cavities.

Question: How can we explain the concept of support to our students?

Respondent 1: Singing "on the breath."

Respondent 2: Support is achieved via a contact with the diaphragm exciting a free flow of air.

Respondent 3: I'm not sure they (the students) realize the total concept. I'm not sure I do. I've heard that correct support is like everything from "feeling like you are having a bowel movement" to filling up a balloon from the bottom first. I know that I have my kids lie down on their backs on the floor and inhale—you have to breathe diaphragmatically, so it gives them the idea of where they have to feel the breath—but I think it really takes much muscle development to have the support one needs to carry over a phrase or have the control we would all want to have.

Respondent 4: Perhaps the most ignorant suggestion made relative to support is "Use your diaphragm." The correct use of muscles involved in the singing process and the correct management of breath will accomplish a supported tone. Numerous exercises are available and can be found in almost any good book on vocal production.

Respondent 5: I give all of my students physical breathing exercises to work on before they ever open their mouths to sing. We get those abdominal muscles moving first, and then we start talking about "mask" and "head" and "chest" resonance. (With young singers, I never even mention "chest" resonance. . . . It is more than enough if they work on getting the sound up front in the mask and bring the head resonance down in to mix with the middle range.)

Respondent 6: My favorite story about support comes from Pablo Elvira when he sang the opening baritone aria in *I Puritani* (with B. Sills) at City Opera. It's a bear of an aria. It opens the show. Tito Capobianco had staged it so that Pablo didn't stay out there to take his applause. Instead he went running into the wings during the ovation. Well, on opening night, the singers in the company knew that Pablo was really geared up for this aria, and we were all watching from the wings. He sang that aria like an angel. He nailed it. Just nailed it. The audience was on their feet, clapping, yelling, "Bravo, bravo!" And Pablo ran into the wings. As he got completely past the legs he put his fists way up in the air, grinned real big, clinched his eyes together, threw his head back, and said, "I love to sing! It's all in the buns!" That's my very favorite story about support.

Respondent 7: I don't think much about that. I just breathe deeply and *sing*.

Respondent 8: Support is created by intake of less breath but under greater pressure.

Question: How does a young singer learn to use support?

Respondent 1: I wish I knew. Maybe I'll learn from your book! I keep hoping someone will introduce me to a foolproof exercise to lock it in.

Respondent 2: Via the tutelage of a fine teacher AND understanding how to activate the back and stomach muscles in the inhalation and exhalation processes.

Respondent 3: Have students stand behind their chairs and lean forward. Then tell them to take a big gasping breath. That forces them to breathe diaphragmatically.

Question: Anything else you would like to add?

Respondent 1: One thing I haven't touched on is pitch, which is a critical problem with so many choral groups, and should be introduced VERY early on. I used to sing flat and never understood why, or even what people were referring to. A helpful concept for me is that the voice should float *on the breath,* even when singing forte. If the singers try to produce a bigger sound by bearing down on their vocal instruments, the pitch can't help but flatten. It's all about singing on the breath. (No one got that across to me for years and years.)

Respondent 2: One of the most valuable assets to the conductor is a knowledge of the sound/gesture relationship. Perfecting all aspects of the conducting technique can be a lifetime study, and a most valuable study for the conductor who has minimal knowledge of vocal technique.

Choral Basics: Exercises

1. Pick a piece of choral music that you plan to rehearse, whether for real or just as an exercise. Develop a five-to-ten-minute warm-up period which prepares the students for that rehearsal. What questions need to be answered before you can even begin to create the warm-ups?
2. Find three pieces that contain an important unison section. These may be in any voicing. Provide all order information: title, composer, arranger/editor, voicing, publisher, octavo number, and price.
3. To check students' understanding of the concept of vowel, diphthong, and consonant pronunciation, a simple exercise will suffice. Choose a lyric and have them write it using vowel sound spellings rather than word spellings. Underline all voiced consonants; circle the few sub-labial (partially voiced) consonants, and write out all diphthongs. A few examples follow.

> My country, 'tis of thee,
> *Mah . . . ee cah . . . uhn tree tihz ahv thee*
>
> sweet land of liberty,
> *soo . . . eet lánd ahv lih b r tee*

of thee I sing.
Ahv thee ah . . . ee sihng

Several practice lyrics are listed below.

Somewhere over the rainbow bluebirds fly.
Birds fly over the rainbow;
why, then, oh why can't I?

Fly me to the moon
and let me play among the stars.
Let me see what spring is like
on Jupiter and Mars.

Holy, holy, holy! Lord God almighty!
Early in the morning
our song shall rise to Thee.

3

THE ACADEMICS OF THE REHEARSAL

A. Teaching Sight-Singing

As musicians, the chances are very good that our backgrounds include some instruction in reading music, whether it was piano lessons while we were very young, or playing in the school bands or orchestras, or singing in choirs. To varying degrees of proficiency, reading music, and in particular reading choral scores, is a skill which has not eluded most of us. The same is not necessarily true of high school choral music students. We should assume that our students, upon entering the choral program, have minimal music reading skills. It is necessary to begin teaching this skill from square one with each new group of students.

A note: This is an expression of honesty. I never learned to sight-sing by any of the various systems. I just "winged it" and found most of the pitches. Having discussed this with a number of my friends, I find it is true with many of them as well. If you need to learn the concept of *solfeggio* with your students, you are not alone, believe me. Before beginning to teach sight-singing skills, several decisions need to be made. First, will there be a text for each day's sight-singing lesson, and will it provide the structure for these lessons? Second, how much time will be devoted to introducing concepts (key signatures, time signatures, note values, and the like), and how much will be spent drilling? Finally, how will different levels be delineated? What will be different from one level to the next?

In the structure provided by a method that I have used, sight-singing is studied daily in class. Students' concept-learning, as well as their drill time, is divided into three levels, according to the level of the choir they are in. Several resources are used for daily drill. At the introductory level, I choose a book that introduces all keys and is excellent for introducing the concept of *solfeggio* (*solfège*), a method often used to teach sight-singing. There are several of these books in print; just look for something that moves very slowly and uses mainly conjunct exercises that are very tonal. If your retailer knows his or her stuff, you can get guidance there.

At an intermediate level, a text is introduced that works not only in unison but in multiple voicings (SA, TTB, SATB, etc.). There are two options for acquiring texts at this level. If you have a healthy choral library, go into the literature and use the music in it. The music can get more sophisticated as the skills improve. A second option is to purchase one of the several published texts which are divided into ability levels. The second level books are perfect for this intermediate singer. I still recommend that the musical activity be mainly conjunct and tonal.

For students in an advanced choir, sight-singing means getting out the hymnals and singing several chorales on *solfège* each day. The second "text" for these advanced students is the music in their folders. Approach a sixteen-bar phrase to be rehearsed that day and practice it on *solfège*. When that point is reached during the choral rehearsal, there are no note learning problems. *Voilà!* Your choir is sight-singing.

Although the concept of *solfège* may not be new to most choral music educators (I red-facedly admit I had never even heard the word *solfège* until my sophomore year in college), a few words to introduce this concept are probably in order.

Very briefly, when using this technique, each diatonic scale tone is assigned one of seven syllables: *do, re, mi, fa, sol, la,* or *ti*. For a fairly extended period of rehearsal time, exercises are limited to the use of these seven syllables, effectively creating sight-singing examples that are completely diatonic. As students find more confidence in singing these diatonic exercises, the use of chromatic tones is introduced. When a given note is raised a half step, either by a sharp or a natural (or in a very few cases even a flat), a variation of the diatonic syllable is used. As shown on the next page, *di, ri, fi, si,* and *li* are the syllables used to express those tones. Note that there is no raised syllable for *mi* or *ti,* as they are already one half step from the next pitch.

When a given note is lowered a half step, either by a flat or a natural (or a sharp if coming from a double sharp), a similar variation of the diatonic syllable is used: *ra, me, se, le,* and *te.* Again, note that the tones that are only one half step below *do* and *fa* are given totally new names; a lowered *do* is *ti,* and a lowered *fa* is *mi.* What follows is a complete *solfège* chart.

	do	
	ti	
te		*li*
	la	
le		*si*
	sol	
se		*fi*
	fa	
	mi	
me		*ri*
	re	
ra		*di*
	do	

For elements such as rhythm-reading, exercises are broken down into their various component parts and are demonstrated individually: first, key and time signatures; second, rhythm; third, pitches; and finally, all combined. This pattern exists for all levels. For a sample lesson in *solfège,* take a look at the following pages.

It is important that the teacher remember that if *solfège* is to lead to the ability to read a score at sight, drill must be regular and the presentation of material must be incremental—that is, each lesson must build on the last. Try never to completely skip the sight-singing lesson, even on days when the choral rehearsal slate is full. This regularity of sight-singing practice will pay off in time saved in teaching notes.

B. Presenting a Basic Sight-Singing Lesson

Although it is possible to learn choral parts by rote—that is, by having someone perform the parts and then parroting that performance—there are several very good reasons why sight-reading parts is preferable to rote-learning. Probably most obvious is the fact that the amount of time spent learning notes in a song is drastically reduced when the singers read their own parts. As a result of saving time the conductor can teach more literature, polish languages to a greater extent, or generally improve any facet of the performance. The final result of spending this extra time polishing the music is that the final performance will probably be more accurate and sound better. All because the singers could read their music.

It is true that in every choral organization there are students who are able to sight-sing without daily lessons. These are usually students in band or orchestra or those who have studied piano. A lot of rehearsal time can be saved by letting these students "lead" their sections. However, there are definite problems with this method of learning/teaching music. First, it is very possible, indeed probable, that such a student will be pegged as a "pet," and, although he or she may be very useful to the choir, the choral experience may be a less positive one for him or her. Second, the leader may hurt his or her voice by singing uncomfortably low or high for the sake of the section. How many young sopranos have (along with cheerleaders) done damage to their vocal cords by singing the alto part because they could read the music? The same can happen in any section where there are perceived weaknesses. A third problem that often arises is that the "leader" often develops a harsh vocal quality due to pushing the sound so that all in the section can hear. A final reason not to expect choirs to learn literature by imitating a member of the section is that the rest of the choir is crippled. They leave the choral setting having learned a bunch of notes, but not having acquired reading skills.

So, where to start? Obviously there is knowledge that needs to be acquired before one can even begin to sight-sing. Clef signs, note types (quarter, half, etc.), key signatures, and time signatures are but a few. These are basic music theory skills, and if the student does not have them upon arrival, it will be necessary to teach them before a sight-singing lesson can begin.

During and after the time in which these basic theory skills are being taught, simple and short examples should be presented to the class. Because the student may just be learning key signatures, time signatures, etc., assumptions will be made regarding these basic knowledges.

First, explain to the students that the note in the first cell of the piece ("called a measure") is a whole note, and often it gets four beats ("taps of the toe"). Have the students clap and count a series of whole notes. Half notes and quarter notes can be introduced in the same manner. Have the class count a variety of patterns of these three notes until they are able to look at the exercise and count and clap it. Explain that the arrangement of numerals at the beginning of the piece tells the performer that a whole note equals four beats, and so on. Do not go into the whys or wherefores at this point.

Once the teacher is confident that all students are able to read those simple whole note, half note and quarter note patterns, it is time to introduce pitches.

If the students come from any sort of middle school/junior high music background, note names have almost certainly been taught. Begin by assuming this, and you will soon learn the extent of the students' preparation. First, have the students recite note names, assigning no rhythmic values to the recitation. If necessary, tell the students the names of the five notes involved. Second, by rote teach the students the *solfège* scale: *do, re, mi, fa, sol, la, ti,* and *do.* Do not be concerned with the spelling of the syllables, just get them into the students' heads. Then present the first half of the example to the class. Tell them the first note is *do,* and ask them to attempt to figure out the other pitch names. After a few false starts and some wise-cracking from at least one boy (Sexist? So be it), most of the students will intuitively choose the correct syllables. For those who don't, briefly explain that once the first tone is identified, one goes forward or backward on the scale, depending on whether the music goes up or down the scale. Have the students chant the syllables first, arrhythmically. Later they can match syllables to note type. In a true beginning group, this may very well fill out the week.

The next step is to match sound to syllable. Give the students the first pitch, and ask them to sing the notes in the first four measures without regard to the rhythm. Once that is achieved, have them combine the elements of rhythm and pitch. Since these two elements were introduced previously, this step will probably go very quickly. Present the rest of the example, and the students have sight-sung. It's a start.

In successive lessons, examples should be taught using the method outlined above. If the teacher chooses, only examples in the key of C will be introduced until the concept of key signatures has been learned. I personally prefer to present examples in several keys so that the students learn immediately that "do" is movable to any pitch of the scale. Singing in several keys works as long as all information is spoon-fed to the student. It is important not to use phrases such as "this example is in the key of F" or "in this key all B's are flatted." When you introduce something new, share the mere skeleton of information pertaining to this new concept. Otherwise, the inevitable questions follow, and they divert all from the task at hand: learning to sight-sing simple melodies and rhythms.

After a month or so of working at this level, it is time to relate the basic theory skills to a melody which is more like the music in the students' folders. Read simple rhythmic patterns and relate them to several different time signatures. Figure out the placement of *do* by relating it to a key signature.

A lot of drill will be necessary to acquire these skills, but once they have been addressed, both teacher and class are ready to apply these basic exercise skills to songs. Keep them simple, no chromaticism or syncopation; try to find tunes composed mainly using conjunct motion.

The process described above is good for a complete year's curriculum in sight-singing. Drill is the essential factor. Don't let a rehearsal go by without some sight-singing drill, even if it is only five minutes' worth. Consistency and time spent on task are keys to learning to sight-sing. Suggestions for sight-singing work at intermediate and advanced levels are included in the previous section.

C. Acquiring Basic Skills in the Choral Classroom

In many choral music classes a lot of notes are learned; a lot of shows are prepared; beautiful music is made; and contests are entered. In some choral classes basic skills of musicianship are learned as well. There is no question that music classes—both choral and instrumental—are expected to serve a utilitarian function within the school and the community. When the PTA sponsors a spaghetti dinner, they may expect strolling strings or vocal selections from light opera. Very few schools are afforded the luxury of sponsoring a band program that is not expected to march in the hometown parades and at the school's football games. When the principal wants carols sung at the Rotary club meeting, the choral music program is expected to provide them. Some school administrations expect a Broadway-style musical, or they revel in winning contests, or they want a madrigal group or a swing choir to serve as public relations elements for the school. These are facts, and they are not negotiable, nor are they necessarily negatives.

If performance activities become the only goals of the choral program, however, then the students in the classes are being offered a less-than-whole experience. In essence, they are being given only a performance-oriented musical experience, and the classes become unnecessary as far as the overall school curriculum is concerned. In some choirs, basic musical skills are being taught as well as basic choral skills. This model of teaching both sets of skills should be in place in every choral music program if it is to be accepted seriously as part of the development of the school curriculum.

Probably the first step toward the acquisition of skills is to decide which skills will be included in the assessment program. Because each teacher values different skills, there will be many different skill areas identified for inclusion. While these various areas are valued, there is a certain group of skills that seem to be more or less universally accepted.

Learning to read music is an important element of the musical experience. To that end, sight-singing should be a main concern in the choral classroom. Three major components of this skill immediately identify themselves: 1) learning types of notes and their rhythmic values, which necessitates learning the concept of time signatures; 2) learning to identify written pitches by name, which necessitates the learning of clef signs; and 3) learning to sight-sing written music. Learning key signatures is a skill that is closely identified with this music-reading goal. It may be considered a separate activity or it may be taught as part of the sight-reading sequence.

Certainly a major part of skill development in music is *learning the language of music*. Basic terms associated with musical performance are elements that cannot be ignored. How does a musician express the loudness or softness of music? Are there terms that tell a performer how to execute a piece of music? For example, how does a performer know to play forcefully or delicately, or short and accented, or smoothly and connected? Are there words that tell how fast or slow a piece is to be performed? The list of terms a student should learn must be developed by the teacher. Although the final product will be very similar from one teacher to the next, the order of presentation will differ from one class to another and from one program to another. Those differences make each individual choral program unique.

Learning the signs and symbols of music is an important skill. Can elements of performance be represented by a symbol? What signs identify tempo and tempo changes? What symbols are used to structure the written score: repeats, endings, and separations? Obviously these are but a few suggestions as to signage; each teacher must develop his or her own lists.

Since this topic is about acquiring skills in the *choral* classroom, it stands to reason that one of the major goals of our teaching should be *tone production and vocal development*. Students should learn basics of the mechanics of tone production and even something about the musculature. Placement, resonance, and a host of other qualities are legitimate targets for student learning. These skills may be best taught using the music being prepared in the classroom as part of the performance goals. Wise warm-ups—carefully explained and executed—can be vehicles for teaching certain skills.

Another skill that can be taught using the music already being studied in class is *score reading*. Much of the information regarding score reading will have been covered in units on language and signs and symbols, but it is also necessary that the student be able to use terms like "system" and "score," to name a couple. This may be the area in which the learner is expected to identify basic formal structures: binary, ternary, sonata, and symphony. These are all terms that the student needs to handle when reading a score. There are also symbols that are unique to the structure of a piece of music, such as *dal segno*, and the symbols which mark measure numbers.

Keyboard proficiency is important in my classroom. The goal is not to teach a student to play piano, but to make it possible for him or her to play a single part to learn notes outside of the classroom. Using keyboard skills to play another part while singing your own is encouraged. Many teachers might not feel this is a valid goal in their classroom. Again, all of these are only suggestions. The content of a program to teach musical skills must be generated by the individual teacher, based on the goals of his or her program. The point is that there needs to be some organized, structured approach to introducing a basic level of musicianship. Only when some sort of program is up and running will choral music take its place in the school curriculum alongside geometry and English composition. And that is where it deserves to be.

The Academics of the Rehearsal: Exercises

1. Pick a piece of music you don't know. For each note in your part, provide the *solfège* syllable.
2. Collect ten books on sight-singing, or which have major sections devoted to sight-singing. Using these as a basis, create an annotated bibliography which you can use and which you can share with others to build a major bibliography.
3. Choose four areas of musical basics that you would like your students to improve in: tone production, diction, language, and so forth. Then, choose four separate tasks under each category and write a description of what the student will be able to do after accomplishing the objective: "The student will sing a pure *ah* vowel"; or "the student will define the following terms: *andante, allegro, and vivace.*"

Using all the skill at your fingertips, draw up an acquisition sheet for each objective and provide all the information necessary to answer the question. For example: "There are a number of terms in music which describe the speed of a piece of music. Terms which tell the conductor the piece is fast are *vivace, presto,* and *leggiero,* to name a few. *Langsam, andante,* and *grave* all denote a slow song. A medium speed is denoted by the terms *allegro* or *moderato* among others.

"So, the definition of *vivace* is: a fast speed for a song.

"The definition of *allegro* is: a medium speed for a song.

"The definition of *andante* is: a slow speed for a song."

The student will be expected to score 100 percent on a fill-in-the-blank quiz.

4

IMPORTANT RELATED TOPICS

A. The Boy's Changing Voice

It was at an ACDA (American Choral Directors Association) convention that I ran into one of my old college buddies. As you will soon learn by your own experience at these conventions, old friendships are rekindled in less time than it takes to read a name tag. Suddenly, instead of talking about the next test or complaining about the last theory lecture, you are talking about the classes you teach, the successes (never the failures) of your choir, and literature, always literature. Perhaps even a lie or two is exchanged. Inevitably, when these subjects have been put to bed, the comment will be made by the middle school person, "At least you don't have to deal with unchanged and changing voices."

Au contraire, my friend.

Perhaps it would be wise before going any further in this discussion to provide some background information. At the schools where I have taught, it has been possible to separate the freshman guys from the freshman girls. This arrangement makes it possible to address with the guys topics such as changing voice, falsetto singing, and increasing the range, in a non-threatening environment. Concepts like chest voice and smoothing out breaks can be discussed and rehearsed with the girls. (Did you know that girls go through a voice change, too? It normally does not need to be addressed because it occurs almost imperceptibly.) All-in-all a very satisfactory arrangement. If, however, you are in a situation where enrollment does not support two freshman choirs, I strongly suggest that you find a way to assign part of the period, or certain class periods, to single-sex learning. Where there's a will there's a way. (I made that up.) In some schools there might be a problem with certain government programs which ended sexual discrimination in scheduling. It should be possible to work it out with your school's curriculum director.

A note about single-sex ensembles in the curriculum: It is fairly simple to define your programs in such a way that the names of ensembles do not interfere with their scheduling. Instead of offering Boys/Girls Chorus, offer Treble Chorus and Bass Chorus. Thus you have established the groups you want by defining them musically, not sexually. I have never encountered a young man who asked to be assigned to the treble ensemble, even if his voice had not changed. I have, however, met several young women who insisted that they were tenors. A brief discussion of the harm that can be done to a young voice when it is pushed to sing too low solves that problem every time.

When first encountering changing or unchanged voices, the teacher's primary objective is to not harm the voice. To make a boy soprano sing tenor could be harmful; to force a boy with a two-note range to sail with the tenors or bottom out with the basses could be harmful; anything that pushes a boy's range beyond its capabilities on a given day could be harmful. Here is where arranging skills come into play. Write a "high" first tenor part for the soprano or alto; find published cambiata voicings or create some of your own for the young man with a severely limited range; and create "low" bass parts for the boy who is stuck in the basement. Above all, keep them singing and keep the singing healthy. It is much better at this stage of development to err on the side of caution than to force the range.

That is not to say that increasing the range should be ignored. It is important to vocalize throughout the range and to encourage the young men to sing as high or low as possible without forcing. Finding and using the falsetto voice is important in this process. And listen to these voices frequently. When you notice appreciable differences in range or tone, react immediately. Write a lower "high" tenor part or lower the "low" bass part. Overall, the key is to know the voice and to react to its changes.

In my experience, these voices most often change according to four specific patterns. However, there are some boys whose voice change is so horrendous that it fits into none of these four categories. I work with them privately on an out-of-school basis. It may be necessary to work with these students on such elementary concepts as matching pitches and differentiating up from down and high from low. We work on the voice until it is functional.

Here are the standard patterns for voice change in adolescent voices:

The high voice (soprano or alto) that changes slightly and slowly to a tenor voice. This is the easiest type of change to work with because no "lumps or bumps" are present to interfere with technically good singing.

The voice that drops all the way to the sub-basement of the range and loses all mid-range. Help the young man find his falsetto voice: it is fairly easy from there to close that gap by rehearsing down from the falsetto into the lower parts of the range.

Some voices lose all highs and lows and are restricted to an incredibly narrow vocal range somewhere around middle C. Hitting this student in the head probably will not help him live through the voice change. Patiently have him vocalize in his "range" and slowly add notes that are higher or lower than "his notes." These will come, but the process is slow.

The final of these most common voice change types is basically the same as the first one, except that it is similar to a high adult voice moving down into a baritone or bass range. This will happen gradually, and there is nothing you should do except work on tone quality and technique. Stay out of his way.

In fact, in retrospect, that might be a pretty good summary of my working with unchanged voices: *stay out of the way.* Help, encourage, work on related skills, and let nature take its course. Voice change can be a painful and painfully slow process for some of these guys; be patient and supportive.

B. Singing in Foreign Languages

One of the most rewarding experiences you can give to your students is that of singing in a language other than English. The pronunciations they use will help them in any language class they take; the few words they pick up could help them in travel; and the sense of accomplishment when the project is finished will undoubtedly enhance self-esteem. Musically, the word accents and vowel sounds (consonants as well) of the original language fit the music much better than an English transcription.

Three languages are most often sung in choral music settings: Latin, French, and German. There certainly will be times when you and the choir will be called upon to sing in a language other than these three; for example, if your school is in an ethnic neighborhood, the choir may be expected to provide entertainment in the native tongue of the area. There are a few other languages which are commonly performed — Russian, for example. The choral music of Borodin and Rachmaninoff, to name only two, is among the standard choral literature.

1. A Pronunciation Guide for Latin

Latin is probably the simplest language for Americans to sing because there are so many similarities between the two languages. All vowels are pure vowels, and they are consistent from one word to the next. Would that English were so consistent.

Table 4.1

---

a is always pronounced *ah* as in *father*
e is always pronounced *eh* as in *set*

Some purists will brighten the *eh* vowel in certain grammatical settings, but the vowel is still *eh*.

i is always pronounced *ee* as in *free*
o is always pronounced *oh* as in *foreign*

The Latin *oh* is more open than ours. It carries with it a touch of *aw*.

u is always pronounced *oo* as in *food*

When two Latin vowels are written together, they do not elide to make a new sound, as in English. Some examples follow.

Mei is pronounced *Meh—ee*, never *May*
Laudamus is pronounced *Lah—oo—da—mus*, never *Loudamus*
Gloria is pronounced *Gloh—ree—ah*, never *Glorya*

Table 4.2. A Pronunciation Guide for Selected Latin Consonants

Letter	Sound	Pronunciation
c before *e, i, ae,* and *oe* is pronounced	*ch*	as in *choose*
c in other situations is pronounced	*k*	as in *cool*
g before *a, o,* and *u* is hard	g	as in *gog*
g before *e* and *i* is soft	*j*	as in *gyroscope*
h is normally silent		
h between two *ll*'s is pronounced as a soft	*k*	as in the Yiddish *chutz-pah*
j and *y* in Church Latin are pronounced	*ee*	as in *see*
ch is pronounced	*k*	as in *cat*
gn is pronounced	*ny*	as in *canyon*
th is pronounced	*t*	as in *tape*
ti before a vowel is pronounced	*ts*	as in *pizza*
cc before *e* and *i* is pronounced	*ch*	as in *church*
xc is pronounced	*ksh*	as in *thick shoe*
A softer sound is produced using	*gsh*	as in *eggshell*

There are a few examples of vowels next to the other in which only one is sounded, due to a function of the grammar. You can deal with them as they come up. One of the most common combinations is *ae* as in *filiae,* which is pronounced as a long *a.*

Most Latin consonants are exactly like their English counterparts, but a few need to be explained (see Table 4.2).

The obvious use for Latin in singing is to sing the music written mainly for the Roman Catholic Church, since Latin was the official language of the Church around the globe until very recently. Because the Latin Mass and other musical forms used in the Church are a mainstay of the choral repertoire, it is very important that conductors know not only pronunciations but also the meanings of the texts their choirs are singing.

Provided below is the text of the Ordinary of the Mass along with its translation; the Ordinary is that part of the Mass which is performed each time the Mass is said. The sections of the Proper of the Mass are those which change from one liturgical occasion to another to reflect the attendant celebration; Christmas, Pentecost, and Lent, for example, require particular texts.

The Text of the Latin Mass as used in Schubert's Mass in G

Kyrie

Kyrie Eleison,	Lord, have mercy on us.
Christe Eleison,	Christ, have mercy on us.
Kyrie Eleison.	Lord, have mercy on us.

Gloria

Gloria in excelsis Deo,	Glory to God in the highest,
et in terra pax hominibus	and on earth, peace to men
bonae voluntatis.	of good will.
Laudamus te, benedicimus te,	We praise you, we bless you,
adoramus te, glorificamus te.	we adore you, and we glorify you.
Gratias agimus tibi	We thank you
propter magnam gloriam tuam.	for your great glory.
Domine Deus, Rex coelestis,	Lord God, King of heaven,
Pater omnipotens, Domine fili,	Father almighty, God the Son,
unigenite, Jesu Christe;	the only begotten, Jesus Christ;
Domine Deus, Agnus Dei,	Lord God, Lamb of God,
Filius Patris,	Son of the Father,
Qui tollis peccata mundi,	Who takes away the sins of the world,
miserere nobis.	have mercy upon us.
Suscipe deprecationem nostram,	Take away our sins,
Qui sedes ad dexteram Patris;	(You) Who sits at the right hand of God;
miserere nobis,	have mercy on us,
Quoniam tu solus sanctus;	You alone are holy;
tu solus Dominus;	You only are God;
tu solus altissimus, Jesu Christe,	You alone are the highest, Jesus Christ,
cum sancto spiritu in gloria	with the Holy Spirit in the glory
Dei Patris. Amen.	of God the Father. Amen.

Credo

Credo in unum Deum,	I believe in one God,
Patrem omnipotentem,	Father all-powerful,

factorem coeli et terrae,
visibilim omnium
et invisibilium.

maker of heaven and earth,
and of everything that can be seen
and (everything) unseen.

Et in unum Dominum
Jesum Christum,
Filium Dei unigenitum,
(et) ex Patre natum,
ante omnia saecula.
Deum de Deo, lumen de lu-
mine,
deum verum de Deo vero;
genitum non factum,
con substantialem Patri,
per quem omnia facta sunt.

And (I believe) in one Lord,
Jesus Christ,
the only Son of God,
(and) born of the Father
before all the ages.
Lord of Lord, light of light,

true God of true God;
born, not made,
of the same substance as the Father,
through Whom all things were
made.

Qui propter nos homines
et nostram salutem
descendit de coelis
et incarnatus est
de Spiritu Sancto
ex Maria Virgine,
et homo factus est.
Crucifixus etiam pro nobis
sub Pontio Pilato,
passus et sepultus est.
Et resurrexit tertia die
secundum scripturas,
et ascendit in coelum,
sedet ad dexteram Patris,

Who for us men
and our salvation
came down from the heavens
and was born again
of the Holy Spirit
from the Virgin Mary.
And He became a man.
Also, He was crucified for us
under Pontius Pilate.
He was dead and He was buried.
And He arose on the third day
as it was written in the scriptures,
and He rose into heaven.
He sits near the right side of the
Father.

et iterum venturus est
cum gloria
judicare vivos et mortuos,
cujus regni non erit finis.
Et in Spiritum Sanctum,
Dominum et vivificantem,

And He is going to come again
with glory
to judge the living and the dead.
His kingdom shall have no end.
And (I believe) in the Holy Ghost,
the Lord and the One who gives
life,

qui ex Patre Filioque proedit,

Who is the product of the Father
and Son.

qui cum Patre et Filio simul adoratur et conglorifica-tur,	Who, with the Father and the Son together, is worshipped and greatly glorified,
qui locutus est per prophetas.	Who was spoken of by the prophets.
(Et unam sanctam catholicam	(And [I believe] in one holy catholic
et apostolicam et ecclesiam.)	and apostolic church.)
Confiteor unum baptisma in remissionem peccatorum,	I confess one baptism for the remission of sins,
(Et expecto resurectionem)	(And I look forward to the resurrection)
mortuorum, et vitam venuri saeculi. Amen.	of those who have died, and the life of the ages to come. Amen.

Sanctus et Benedictus

Sanctus, sanctus, sanctus, Dominus Deus Sabaoth, pleni sunt coeli et terra gloria tua.	Holy, holy, holy, Lord God of the hosts, heaven and earth are full of Your glory.
Osanna in excelsis.	Hosanna in the Highest.
Benedictus qui venit in nomine Domini.	Blessed is he that comes in the name of the Lord.
Osanna in excelsis.	Hosanna in the highest.

Agnus Dei

Agnus Dei Qui tollis peccata mundi,	Lamb of God Who takes away the sins of the world,
miserere nobis; dona nobis pacem.	have mercy on us; give us peace.

Even though it may seem to be a daunting task, it is very important that the conductor should know the meaning of the text—word for word.

2. A Pronunciation Guide for German

The cantatas of Bach, the motets of Brahms, and the glorious music of Beethoven; you won't have to look far to find these texts translated into English. And it is probable that you can find a translation which is relatively accurate. But word accuracy alone isn't enough when recreating the music of these masters. You have to consider the word accents, the consonant and vowel sounds as they paint the text, and the splendid sounds unique to the German language. Baroque text rhythm is based on the production of explosive consonants in performance. These are only a few of the reasons why many conductors choose to perform German music using its original language. Your students will be much richer if they have had the experience of singing the music of these composers as they intended it.

As in Latin, most consonants in German are pronounced the same as their English counterparts. Some exceptions are listed in Table 4.4.

3. A Guide to French Pronunciation

French choral compositions are important additions to every choral library. From the earliest chant, through medieval motets, in each of the major compositional periods up to the twenty-first century, the French heritage is very rich. Certainly the music of the Impressionistic period is important to all choral musicians (even if they choose to ignore the music of the Burgundian or Flemish schools). The music of Fauré, Poulenc, and Debussy alone make at least an acquaintance with French pronunciation a necessity for the choral singer.

The French pronunciation guide in Table 4.5 is based on the Web site *Babel Site: The Language Page*, by Dàvid Uhlár: http://perso.wanadoo.fr/babel-site/french.htm. Don't miss his disclaimer at the end of the guide.

From the author of the pronunciation guide: "Don't be bothered by all the rules. There are many more in French. (We even say that we have an impossible language to write and to pronounce.) Like in English, the French spelling system is a bit strange, and we can

Table 4.3. A Pronunciation Guide for Selected German Vowels

Letters		Sound	Pronunciation
a, aa, ah	are pronounced	*ah*	as in *father*
ä, äh	are pronounced	*eh*	as in *fair*
ae, aeh	are pronounced	*a*	as in *cat*
ai, ay	are pronounced	*i*	as in *my*
au	is pronounced	*ow*	as in *mountain*
eu	is pronounced	*oi*	as in *spoil*
e	is usually pronounced	*eh*	as in *chest*
e	in prefixes (*ge-*, *be-*) is pronounced	*uh*	as in *about*
ee, eh	are pronounced	*ay*	as in *play*
ei	is pronounced	*i*	as in *my*
i	is usually pronounced	*ee*	as in *see*
i	in some other cases is pronounced	*ih*	as in *hit*
ie	is pronounced	*ee*	as in *please*
ih	is pronounced	*ih*	as in *little*
o	is usually pronounced	*aw*	as in *law*
o	before certain consonants (e.g., *C*) in final syllables is pronounced	*oh*	as in *boat*
ö	has no English equivalent.		Form an *oh* shape with lips; sing an *eh* through it.
u	is usually pronounced	*oo*	as in *who*
ü	has no English equivalent.		Form an *oo* shape with lips; sing *ee* through it.

Note: Almost all vowels, when they precede the combination *cc*, are performed in their most open form.

use several letters to write a single sound! Imagine: *oiseaux* (English 'birds') is pronounced /wazo/: 8 letters for 4 sounds! And *eaux* (English 'waters') is simply pronounced /o/."

Much of the world's greatest choral literature is written in languages other than English. Give your students the opportunity to experience this music in its native tongue.

Table 4.4. A Pronunciation Guide for Selected German Consonants

Letter	Sound	Pronunciation
b at the end of a word or syllable is pronounced	*p*	as in *put*
ch is often pronounced	*ch*	as in *chutzpah*
ks is pronounced	*ks*	as in *books*
d at the end of a word or syllable is pronounced	*t*	as in *hat*
g at the end of a word or syllable is usually pronounced	*k*	as in *cat*
j is pronounced	*y*	as in *yes*
qu is pronounced	*kv*	as in *kvell*
s before a vowel is pronounced	*z*	as in *as*
sch, and *s* before *p* and *t*, are usually pronounced	*sh*	as in *shoe*
ß is pronounced	*s*	as in *sit*
v is pronounced	*f*	as in *fame*
w is pronounced	*v*	as in *value*

C. Popular Choral Music

This entry in my collection of thoughts is, I admit from the beginning, completely subjective. The views expressed are my own (I feel like I am writing the disclaimer at the beginning of *The Jerry Springer Show*), and they should not be accepted as choral dogma. I am encouraged that many other choral directors feel the same way.

America is rich in the variety, quantity, and quality of its popular music. It will serve no purpose here to study the development of the art form and its many derivatives. If, however, you plan to perform popular choral music in your ensembles, it would behoove you to undertake such a study. What I believe is supremely important in performing this music is *style*. The beginnings of understanding style will emerge from a knowledge of the history of this art form.

Note: Throughout this discussion, I will use the term *popular* to include all forms of lighter choral fare. I will use the term *pop* when writing about musical theater repertoire and standard contemporary

Table 4.5 A Pronunciation Guide for Selected French Vowels and Consonants

a, â, à are pronounced	*ah*	as in *father*
an, en, am, em, aon are pronounced	*an*	as in *tarnish*
(This is an approximation of a sound not in the English language)		
é is pronounced	*ay*	as in *date* (no diphthong)
ê, è, ai are pronounced	*eh*	as in *fair*
eu, oeu are pronounced	*er*	as in *pleasure*
(This is an approximation of a sound not in the English language)		
i is pronounced	*ee*	as in *meet*
in, im are pronounced	*a* (nasal)	
(This is an approximation of a sound not in the English language)		
o, ô, au, eau are pronounced	*oh*	as in *boat* (no diphthong)
o is also pronounced	*ah*	as in *hot*
on, om are pronounced	*o* (very nasal)	
(This is an approximation of a nasal sound not in English)		
ou is pronounced	*oo*	as in *food*
oi is pronounced	*w*	as in *water*
u, û, ù are pronounced	*ee*	through an *oo* mouth position, as in German *küsse*
(This is an approximation of a sound not in the English language)		
un, um	are pronounced *a* (nasal)	
(This is an approximation of a nasal sound not in English)		
c before *e* and *i* is pronounced *s*		as in *city*
c is pronounced	*k*	as in *cat*
ç is pronounced	*s*	as in *sit*
ch is pronounced	*sh*	as in *shoe*
g before *e* and *i* is pronounced	*zh*	as in *pleasure*
g is pronounced	*g*	as in *gutter*
gn is pronounced	*ny*	as in *Kenya*
h is silent		
j is pronounced	*zh*	as in *azure*
r is		"ticked" as in the German *Herr*
(This is an approximation of a sound not in the English language)		
s normally sounds like	*s*	as in *sit*
s at the end of a word is silent		
x is pronounced	*ks*	as in *six*
x at the end of a word is silent		

fare. Jazz and gospel will describe the other two art forms in these pages.

If your ensemble performs a ballad from the "standards" repertoire, something like "Unforgettable," it is important that its sound, its inflections, and its articulations be different from those in a selection from *The Phantom of the Opera*. The way to learn these differences is to *listen*. Listen to musicals from the early part of the twentieth century. (*No, No, Nanette* is a good one.) Listen to the music of the Depression, such as "Brother, Can You Spare a Dime?" Listen to the big band sound of the '40s and '50s, and trace it to other jazz styles. Listen to rock and roll in its various incarnations. Go back at least as far as *Oklahoma* and listen to the changes in the American musical theater repertoire as it metamorphosed into *Rent* and *Dr. Jekyll and Mr. Hyde*.

As you listen, you will become more discriminating, and what once sounded like "that light music" will begin to take on a history, a progression of development. These are the changes that must be reflected in the performances of pop music by your various ensembles. It simply is not good enough to throw in a pop piece to appease your audience or your singers. If you are going to do it, do it right. You would and should give no less to Mozart.

Another reason to develop discrimination in these styles is to make it possible for you to separate the junk (a lot) from the gems (very few) that we are offered. It is not my intention to bad-mouth either publishers or their arrangers. These folks produce what we buy. If we are to expect good fare from them, then we need to buy the good fare from them. It is, I believe, that simple. There are magnificent arrangements of music from all popular styles; and yes, in my opinion these include rock and roll in all its forms. Unfortunately, in our desire to produce an award-winning performance, we often settle for poor arrangements of boring Top 40 tunes because good arrangements of the great Top 40s are harder to find.

This discussion needs to go no further. Remember to perform only good music, and perform it in a stylistically accurate manner. And perform it well. We are, as we enter this profession, musicians who have chosen to educate young people using the language of music. Whether we are singing music of the Baroque period or a tune recorded by a group in the twenty-first century, we are teaching choral music. Tone quality, diction, interpretation, etc. are all equally important. As in a Brahms motet, the voice must never be forced or strained. Techniques of good singing must prevail over microphones, movement, costume or light shows, and all the other ancillary factors which can make these performances a treat for the singer as well as the audience.

What has been written so far applies to both jazz and pop music. As with pop, listen to jazz and make sure your singers do likewise. Learn the techniques associated with scat singing from the masters of it: Ella Fitzgerald and Sammy Davis, Jr., to name only two in a world of talent.

As in pop music, the jazz of Dixieland sounds different from the jazz of The Real Group. Let those differences be reflected in your performances. Also, don't buy bad arrangements just because they come out in that publisher's packet. There are more good arrangements in print from the jazz repertoire than are available for pop styles, but it is still essential that you be a wise consumer. Looking for a particular tune? Don't settle for the first arrangement you see. Dig until you find the one that is just right.

After many years of insisting that jazz choral music must be acoustic, I have become convinced that the use of microphones is an important component of these performances. Call me a slow learner. However, I still feel that these mikes must not become crutches used to mask poor tone quality or technique. It is the presence they add that is important, and is important to the creation of that stylistically correct sound. If you are not proficient in the use of a sound system, choose a technician to be an integral member of the group. His or her presence will save you hours of frustration.

While not inherently a style of popular choral music, gospel music and perhaps spirituals should be addressed here. I happily admit to being a fan of this music, but only as a consumer. I have never been involved in reproducing these masterpieces, either as a performer or a conductor, but, oh, the joy and the excitement that is generated by a stellar gospel performance. I am convinced that the principles discussed above hold true for gospel music. It must, above all, be performed in the correct style. Do you have to be African-

American to sing gospel? Absolutely not, but as with all of these art forms, familiarity with the style is utmost in recreating it. If you have been raised on the music of the Beatles, and on Sunday mornings sang "Holy, Holy, Holy" in E-flat all your life, it will be more difficult for you to recreate the appropriate style than it is for those who were reared singing this music in their churches and homes from the time they could speak. It's just another form of listening.

To help fill the gaps in your formal training in gospel style, begin to listen to gospel, all gospel—whether a Thomas Dorsey (not the band leader) tune or an improvised melody. Listen and learn.

I have attended a number of workshops and seminars sponsored by ACDA and various music educators' associations, and the chances are good that you will have the same opportunity in your area. Attend them and pick the brains of the experts who lead these sessions. One of the most exciting sessions I ever attended was one led by a local musician, Dr. Keith Hampton, in which he spent a half hour teaching a bunch of very white music teachers from middle America how to sing "What a Friend We Have in Jesus" in gospel style. We weren't good, but we learned, and the final result was a decent stab at singing in the style. As is true with jazz and pop, study development. Understand the influence of "My Lord, What a Mornin' " on "Just a Closer Walk."

An aside: To hear a host of gospel styles in one performance, listen to *A Soulful Messiah,* a fairly recent recording of the Christmas section of Handel's *Messiah* using gospel settings sung by genuine top performers in the gospel field.

Don't forget two things when addressing the reality of performing pop, jazz, or gospel music. First, pieces in these styles should be only one facet of a balanced choral music program. A student who goes through high school singing only jazz, pop, or gospel is as crippled musically as the one who graduates having sung only Schubert. Balance. Second, when working with young voices, your first concern is to do no harm. Much of the bad "rap" that those of us who do these styles receive from our more serious peers is due to misuse of the voice to achieve a specific style. The potential for doing harm is very real in all of these styles; it is so tempting to direct the sopranos to stay in chest voice those extra couple of steps for the sake of the development of a phrase. And it is very possible that the phrase will sound best if it is belted to the end. Sometimes, however, a phrase must suffer so that a voice doesn't.

Perform quality arrangements of quality music in a stylistically correct manner, and at the same time protect young voices. It's a daunting task, but your choral program will prosper when it includes this wonderful music.

Important Related Topics: Exercises

1. Write a short paper on the advantages and disadvantages of singing in a foreign language. Use musical examples to substantiate your various assertions, both negative and positive.
2. Go through all the resources at your disposal and pick out ten pop arrangements, ten jazz charts, ten gospel tunes, and ten Top 40–style pieces which would be worthy of programming on a concert you plan to present to an auditorium full of choir directors. Make sure you differentiate distinctly between the styles; don't, for example, let a purely Top 40 piece slip into your pop group.

5

THE EXTRACURRICULAR PROGRAM

A. So You Are Going to Do a Musical

The production of a Broadway-style musical has become somewhat of a given in many schools over the past twenty years or so; unfortunately the preparation of young teachers to direct these productions has *not* become a given over the past twenty years or so. Most colleges (as they believe they should) spend most of their teacher preparation time in teaching the soon-to-be-teacher to analyze, to conduct, to write lesson plans, to teach to standards—in fact, just about everything except to prepare popular music and musical theater. That is unfortunate because most school corporations are going to expect two things from their choral music departments: 1) programs of a light nature to perform at the local Rotary luncheons, and 2) a musical to be presented either in the fall between the end of the football season and the beginning of the basketball season or in the spring after the boys' basketball season.

How is it possible for a music teacher who has never been taught to put together a musical to undertake such a huge task? The answer, though daunting in its scope, is really rather simple. Don't rely on the college curriculum to prepare you in this area. As it is, most students are challenged to "get through" the program in four years; for many it is impossible. To add even more requirements will further strain that drive toward graduation. Instead of expecting the college to provide this training, get out and perform; learn on your own through experience. Try out for a summer stock job for next to no pay. If stock isn't an option, get involved with community theater or audition for your school's productions. If your musical theater talent is not developed enough, paint sets, pull curtains, learn lighting and sound. All of these are precious skills you will need when your time comes to direct a show.

What if, however, you already have a job, and the time is past for college shows and "my dad has a barn and my mom can make the costumes"? (If you are too young to understand that reference, go immediately to the video store and rent five Judy Garland/ Mickey Rooney musicals.) Here are a few tips that might prove helpful.

First of all, *get help!* Do not try to put together a show on your own. Even a seasoned professional is incapable of adequately tending to all the aspects of a musical show. Hopefully the drama director will do the stage direction for you; if approached correctly, the band and orchestra director may also enjoy being a part of the show. (In other words, do not assume that the "band man" will automatically want to fill the role of musical director for the show.) With any luck, there will be an English teacher or a shop teacher or an art teacher (or anyone else with a flair for designing and building a set) who can fill the role of technical director. Once these three people are chosen, you are one person short of a committee to be the backbone of this project. The final member of this "inner circle" is a producer. More about the producer's duties will follow. The committee's first job will be to provide input on the selection of a show, and that decision may very well be the most important one made during the entire venture. Based on the available talent (remember that phrase for later) *you* should select six or seven shows that fit your needs. Gratefully accept the input of the other committee members, but make the final decision yourself. Then order scripts and scores for the committee to read and study.

The provision of these perusal scripts and scores is one of the most valuable services that you will be offered. Each show is represented by a major lending library. In their publicity brochures, which you will receive *ad nauseam*, there will be request forms for perusal copies. All of the lending libraries offer this service, to varying degrees of satisfaction. Some will provide you with full scripts and scores. Others will provide lead sheets. Still others will provide full orchestral scores, if requested. Although it is never wise to judge a book by its cover, the quality of perusal services offered pretty much tells you about the general quality of the service you will receive from the lending library. The names and addresses of the major lending libraries are provided in Appendix C.

Now to address that phrase—"based on the available talent"— used earlier. This phrase must not be understood to promote pre-casting. To pre-cast a show or to pick a show for a given student in a public school setting is not only highly unethical but may also prove to be very unwise. What is necessary is that you pick shows that you know you can cast from among your students. If you think you have a perfect person to do the role of Maria in *The Sound of Music,* that's terrific, but you had better have two or three other students who could perform that role, not only because it is important for you to have options in casting, but also because that "perfect Maria" may decide she needs to work at Dog 'n' Suds to make money for college. You could be left standing with egg on your face.

Now, back to the subject at hand, choosing a show. Once scripts and scores have been ordered and have arrived, a couple of months should be allowed for the committee to read the shows and study the scores. Get to know the characters. Consider your talent pool; are there students who could play the major roles? Make sure the roles are covered two or three deep, if possible. Then your conscience is clear of any feelings of favoritism. Believe me, you will be accused of that sin often enough during your tenure. Check vocal ranges. If you are considering *The King and I,* it would be foolhardy to select that show if there were no tenors available to sing the role of Lun Tha. If your talent in a given year lies mainly in the men it would not be wise to consider doing *Sweet Charity.* And don't forget to consider the chorus and dance needs. If you are going to look at *West Side Story,* you had better have not only good singers but a group of very fine male and female dancers.

You should go through each of these scripts and scores and make generous notes about each; ask the committee to the best of their ability to do the same. Then get together and talk. Talk about the characters; talk about the plot; talk about the music; talk about offensive language; talk about inappropriate story lines. (Make sure the members of your committee are in touch with the attitudes of the community you serve.) After hearing all of their input, thank them very much, and then make the final selection yourself. The ultimate success or failure of the show is on your head, so the selection of the show should be, finally, yours. This entire selection process should be finished at least a month before auditions begin—earlier, if possible.

During this time period and until the show is presented, you should be adding members to the directorial group to fill roles such as prop manager, costume manager, and others who will supervise the specific areas necessary for putting the show together. These people should be ready to go into action as soon as the name of a show is announced.

Once the show has been selected, the next step is to secure the rights to perform that show. This is done through a contract with the lending library that represents that show. You will need to provide the library with all of the general information about your school (address, phone number, principal's name, etc.) and a few specifics (name of show, dates of production, size of performance facility, expected audience size, price of admission). Based on this information you will receive a contract for two separate fees.

The *royalty* fee is that which is paid to the copyright holders for permission to perform their show. The *rental* fees are those associated with the actual use of rehearsal material. An application for this contract is probably available on the Internet; it is definitely available by mail. Sit down before you look at the money figures; they are going to be big. In fact, royalty and rental fees will make up a major part of your budget.

A specific show has been chosen, and the contract for presentation has been returned to the lending library along with whatever they require in the way of a deposit—purchase order or cash. The first order of business now is to get with the person who will serve as producer of the show and set up a budget. This producer's main jobs will be non-musical and non-theatrical. A student activities type or a business type would make a good producer. My personal feeling is that the producer should be a school staff member. He or she should be comfortable with finances and be able to supervise publicity, ticket printing, poster design and printing, program preparation, and ticket sales. It's a big job, but it is not among the most time-consuming of the various staff positions. Together the two of you must set up a budget for the production of your show. The major expenditures will be as follows:

Royalty
Rental of rehearsal materials
Set construction and painting
Costumes
Set decoration and properties
Make-up
Publicity
Lighting
Sound

The members of your committee should reflect this budget structure. These people will submit budget requests for their areas to the producer. Once an overall budget is devised, they must oversee all spending.

At the risk of sounding elementary, the way to figure this budget is very simple: make a conservative estimate of your total attendance and multiply that by the amount charged per ticket. That dollar figure, plus whatever your school or district plans to invest, is the total amount you can spend on the show. Unless your school district is extremely generous and extremely forgiving, do not exceed this amount. Once you have a preliminary estimate of expenditures from each committee chair (or make it yourself, if you don't have a chair for that area yet), the resultant figure will be approximately five times more than your budget allows. The producer and you will need to make judgment calls at that point regarding the various requests. A budget should be in place before the auditions begin.

A word about salaries: This topic will be handled differently in each setting. Some schools pay for all certified staff members involved, but not for outside help. Some pay for all; some for none. Any system will work; make sure you know in advance what the plan is. It is your responsibility to make whatever system is in place work for you so there are no surprises.

The first activity involving students is the audition. If you are on a limited rehearsal schedule, and if you expect a large turnout, it may be best if you provide students music to sing and readings to present in advance of the actual audition. If, on the other hand, you expect to audition a smaller number of students and your rehearsal period is relaxed, let the students pick the music of their choosing and perhaps even furnish their own monologues. It will be to everyone's advantage if a sheet is prepared in advance describing each major and minor character, listing their vocal ranges, explaining chorus and dance requirements, and listing any specialty assignments (must do gymnastics, be able to polka, speak with a French accent). A lot of questions can be avoided by providing this information in advance. Then take your time listening to these students read and sing.

Cut the number and continue auditioning. Cut again, if necessary to correctly cast the show. Have the choreographer run dance auditions either separately or before or after reading and singing auditions. (*Personal opinion: Every student who auditions for the show should do a dance audition.*) After, and only after, you feel very confident of your decisions, announce the cast and immediately hold a rehearsal for the entire cast to distribute rehearsal materials and to read and sing through the show.

Before going to the next step in the preparation of the show, it would be good to pause here and discuss "audition fallout." It will happen to greater or lesser degrees after each audition you hold until the day you retire. Students and their parents will call you and your bosses to complain about the casting just completed. It matters not whether you have cast a musical or selected a soloist for a four-bar stint in the middle of an anthem. There will always be those who find a personal slight in your selections. Hopefully each person hearing the auditions will have taken notes and you will have kept all audition sheets. Then, if you are confident that this show has been cast honestly and to the best of your ability, provide suggestions based on these collected comments, be a polite listener, and thank the detractor for his or her time. If there is still anger, and if the caller wants to go higher up to complain, politely provide the phone numbers of both the principal and the show's producer. Don't let a hint of irritation enter your voice. You must, at all costs, stay above this sort of game-playing. AND NEVER, NEVER, NEVER TALK TO SOMEONE WHO WISHES TO REMAIN ANONYMOUS. If they don't care enough to identify themselves so that you are able to discuss a specific child, then their only goal is to harass you, and you don't need that.

The next set of decisions you need to make is about rehearsals. Where should they be held? When should they be held? How long will each rehearsal last? How many weeks will the rehearsal period be? These are a few of the questions you need to answer. My personal feelings are that rehearsals should not interfere with the intact choral music curriculum. I fully understand that there are school situations where outside rehearsals are absolutely impossible to schedule. In those cases, you do what you gotta do. However, it is my preference to work for several hours after school. *All of this information should be provided to each cast member before the actual rehearsal period begins.*

Whatever schedule you are on, it is imperative that the three major elements of the stage presentation—music, drama, and dance—work simultaneously. To accomplish this, these three directors need to sit down midweek and set up the next week's rehearsal schedule and have it in the students' hands on Friday. A week's schedule might look like this:

	Mon	*Tues*	*Wed*	*Thurs*	*Fri*
Drama	Stage I.1	Review I.1	Stage I.2,3	Stage I.4	Review I.1–4
	Need James	Same folk	J, L, G, A	Chorus	J, L, G, A, Cho
	and Laurie				
Music	Chorus 3–5	Chorus 3–5	L 3–3:30	J 3–3:30	Entire Cast
	Leads 5–6			Chorus 4–6	all together
Dance	Lead Dancers	Ditto	Chorus 3–6	Off	All together

If students have these schedules in their hands before the week begins, and if the work ethic of never missing a rehearsal is observed, six weeks should be plenty to lead you into the final week of rehearsals and performances. Here is a model for that week.

Thursday and Friday before opening: All singers rehearse with orchestra. No other rehearsals are held those two days.

Saturday before opening: Technical rehearsals on stage to incorporate props, lights, sound, set, and (if it's not too crazy) costumes. This is a tedious rehearsal full of starts and stops when the tech director and his crew set all light and sound cues, work scene changes and generally put the show onstage. Little performing is done by the cast, and the entire day is required.

Sunday before opening: Run the show twice, once with piano, no costumes, and minimal stops. This is a tech polishing rehearsal. After a dinner break, return to school and run the entire show with all components for the first time. Expect it to be rough, but hope for some wonderful surprises.

Monday and Tuesday before opening: The tech crew needs the afternoon to get things in order. That time is available to the three stage directors for trouble areas. After dinner, do a complete dress rehearsal.

Opening Night: It's been a hard week; give the kids a break until call time, which should be at least two hours before the show (at least the first couple of nights).

In a nutshell, the above is a committee structure and a rehearsal schedule structure. If it works for you, please use it. In Appendix D there are two timelines that may be helpful to you. The first is a six-month timeline, showing the progress of the entire planning and rehearsal period. The second is a close look at a schedule for "tech week," that period which is a countdown to performance.

Be prepared for some phone calls from parents whose students are tired, or are not getting their homework done. As long as you are doing exactly what you have promised, the fact is that you are leaving plenty of time for students to recreate and to study. As before, be polite, but make no concessions.

Above all, remember: If the musical cannot be an educational experience, it should not be done. When the choice of a musical is based on school administration desires, or community and audience response alone, this entire time-consuming, student-exhausting, teacher-draining process accomplishes absolutely nothing for the students' educations. I'll give an example of a program of high school musical theater gone wrong.

The committee chose *Cats* as the musical with no regard to the talents of the individuals who would probably audition—mistake #1. The vocal music director had to rewrite all of the chorus and many of the solo spots because the cast for *Cats* is of necessity primarily made up of dancers, not singers—mistake #2. The technical director was not capable/interested in building such an ambitious set, so this set was rented—mistake #3. The choreographer did a beautiful job of recreating the original Broadway choreography—mistakes #4 and #5, and professionals were hired to do sound and lighting—mistake #6. A look at the mistakes I perceive shows this:

#1. When the probable talent pool is not considered in choosing a show, there is a very real risk that all roles cannot be satisfactorily filled.

#2. If the kids can't sing at least most of the music as written, then it might have been wiser to choose a musical which stretches, but does not overwhelm their abilities.

#3. Building a set, even a fairly simple one, is an integral part of the educational aspect of producing a musical show. Kids without the type of talent necessary to work on stage must have the opportunity to work backstage. These jobs are as important as the job of the person who performs the role of Rum Tum Tugger.

#4. The Broadway choreography in a show is the work of a creative artist or team. To perform their choreography without their permission is plagiarism as certain as is lifting a quote without giving credit in a term paper.

#5. In a huge dance show like *Cats,* the original choreography is way out of the talent level of the majority of the students. Again, if you can't do it right, why do it?

#6. See #3.

All of this, upon re-reading, sounds potentially like a call for mediocrity and the production of pap. Nothing could be further from the truth. It is, rather, a call for educational accountability in all parts of our program, including the production of a musical.

I realize that this chapter brings you right to the area where you feel you need the most help, and there it stops. Unfortunately, teaching a person to direct a show is an entire book of its own, or several semesters of classes geared toward acting and directing. The best advice I can give in this setting is to study your script and score religiously, then transfer the picture that is in your head onto the stage.

One last note: Don't let the musical become an extension of your ego, something to give you bragging rights at the next district meeting. Remember it's all for the students.

B. Travel, Parent Groups, and Competition

These three topics are so intertwined that it is almost useless to discuss one without referring to the other two. To travel, a group usually needs parental support. The purpose of travel is often to compete.

Let's start with competition. In and of itself, there is absolutely nothing wrong with competition. Preparing for a contest can hone a group's skills; it can cause the students to work hard to perform at a higher level than at a home concert; it can introduce students to the work of other groups; and it can give the program a focus or goal for a given period of time. If your choir is chosen the winner of the competition, the pride shown by group members is worth every ounce of sweat put into rehearsals and every candy bar sold to raise money.

There are also negatives. A lot of contests are hardly more than rubber stamps for getting trophies. I once took my choir to a "high-powered" competition held in Washington, D.C. When we arrived, all decked out in our performance costumes (even down to polished shoes), prepared to sing our best to represent our school and our community, we found that we were one of only two choirs who had paid their money to take part in this contest. The contest was held in the auditorium of a suburban high school—while school was in session, giving it the feel of one of our daily rehearsals. Did we feel special or what? We should never have assumed that because we had heard the company was reputable and because its brochure listed outstanding choral musicians as judges that our experience would reflect the hype. I never again made the mistake of going into a competition blindly. The goal of the companies that sponsor these activities is money, seldom art. Find the very few that can take the one to foster the other. Happily, they do exist.

It is my opinion that when deciding to compete, it is best to find a competition that tests your choir's musical skills as well as its performance skills. There are contests in which sight-reading is a portion of the judging. Some require that a thorough warm-up be a part of the presentation, to give the judges examples of tone quality, vowels, and other choral basics. Others include a question and answer session between the choir and the judges so they can more accurately evaluate the group.

My personal "beef" with competition is that some choirs have completely abandoned their quest for choral excellence in favor of learning a single presentation and spending the better part of a semester or even a year perfecting it. The final product is usually spectacular, but at what cost to the students' aesthetic development? Of course, there are the trophies.

A contest that has excellent judges, offers interesting and inspiring venues, tests the whole gamut of the choir's preparation, and does not cost an arm and a leg to attend can be a wonderfully rewarding, educational venture. Taking part in such competition will undoubtedly be a positive force for your program.

The travel to and from competitions is another topic that has two very different sides. Travel to exciting places is a wonderful experience for youth and adults alike. Make sure when you travel with your ensemble that there is a reason for the travel. One terrific experience my staff and I try to offer our students when we travel is the opportunity to visit universities along the way. While at these colleges, we work in a seminar-style setting with outstanding choral conductors, and sometimes we work in choral music education methods and conducting classes to "pay" for the clinician's time. Usually we have been asked to serve as a demonstration choir for the college students. Sometimes we function as a conductors' choir to provide the students the opportunity to work with a high school choir, teaching us a new piece or working with music in our folders. The advantage to our singers is the opportunity to work with both acknowledged leaders in the field of choral music and also their students. The experience benefits all those involved. (Sometimes the experience with the students is more beneficial than the time with the conductor.)

Another option we have found is the many outstanding festivals that offer performance and evaluation opportunities without the presence of a contest. Often, truly outstanding musicians listen to performances and then spend a considerable amount of time doing a clinic with the choir. The results of these experiences are usually very positive and useful to the choir's development.

In certain instances, there can be a place for travel for its own sake. Travel during school breaks can be included in your group's schedule. These trips can give the students a unique opportunity to learn cooperation and improve their group dynamics. It can give you the opportunity to enjoy the company of your students and to learn about them as people, not merely as students. It is absolutely essential that school officials and parents be aware of the goals of such excursions.

Often a trip can be used as a thank-you to your ensemble members for working hard and achieving the musical goals set out for them. For example, a trip to a major theme park, with a performance scheduled in that park or another can be a wonderful experience for director and singers alike. The students get a chance to show off their performance skills to audiences that enjoy and appreciate the "show." Be careful. There are tour companies that promise wonderful performance venues that become walk-by performances in a local shopping center. An experience like that can ruin an entire trip.

Probably the major criticism of travel is the "let's-take-a-trip-because-we-always-do-and-this-year's-has-to-be-better-than-last-year's-or-the-kids-will-quit-choir" syndrome. First of all, if your program's enrollment is dependent on any non-musical component such as travel, there had better be some re-evaluation of the role of the choral music program in the high school curriculum. Second, there may be years when the school calendar does not easily accommodate a trip. There may be years, God forbid, when terrorist activities forbid excessive travel. The events of September 11, 2001, wrecked school travel plans all over the country. If we are completely honest with ourselves, we know that there are years when travel time could be used more profitably for a different purpose.

A warning and an endorsement: Travel agencies range from good to poor and from ethical to downright dirty. Shop carefully for a company which will provide you the services you desire at a cost you can afford. Housing doesn't necessarily have to be in a four-star hotel, but it also shouldn't be in a hovel. Know in advance what your accommodations will be. The same goes for any performance venues that may be scheduled. It is very possible that your tour planner will not have a musical background; check out all performances that are scheduled in advance. When possible, take the trip you anticipate before the students do. Often travel agencies will pay for this familiarization trip. Sometimes they will provide a trip for a director and a head chaperon. Certain travel agencies do an excellent job of providing you with exactly what you want at the price you can afford. Others want your money and will tell you anything you want to hear. After the trip you will never see them again. As has been cautioned before, do your homework.

Finally, should your choir have a parental support group? My personal feeling is that it should. Interested parents can provide financial support for your program; they can take fundraising worries off your shoulders; they can serve as chaperons when needed; they can help you plan and execute many of your extracurricular activities.

The key concept in all of this is that they *help* you. It is not uncommon for a parent group to become so powerful that they begin to make decisions that are (or should be) the director's to make. Travel is an excellent example. A parent group can be very helpful when you decide to take a trip. The parents can help raise funds, and they can help you with the logistical nightmares of shepherding a group of students. In truth, they can serve in many more capacities to support you. However, sometimes a parent organization forgets its essential duty, one of support, and starts to become a decision-making body. They may want to make the decision as to travel destination; they may want to choose the performance venues.

There could be a hundred things that they "demand" of student musicians. They may even begin to make musical decisions: What style of music should be performed? When should concerts be scheduled? What should be the criteria for giving grades? At this point you have a group that has forgotten its prime directive. There is no way (in my singular opinion) to get this horse back into the barn. Disband the group and re-establish it four years later, when most vestiges of the past group are gone.

A quick discussion about discipline while traveling. I have traveled with groups in which the discipline is so tight and rigid that there is no possible way the students could have a good time. I have also traveled with groups whose disciplinary standards are so low that both the director and the school are at risk because of the possibility of an accident or some unacceptable activity during the trip. There is a middle ground, and it is essential that you find it.

Travel with plenty of chaperons, and set up your trip so that each of them takes responsibility for a specific group of students. That assures that each singer has a surrogate parent for the duration. If you don't want to be up at all hours of the night checking on the whereabouts of students, hire a security service to roam the halls all night.

Finally, travel with a nurse. He or she will be worth any cost to you.

So . . . Attend an educationally exciting contest or festival; have parents in charge of raising the money and providing the support services; and hire a travel agent who is a musician and completely ethical to plan your trip at a reasonable cost. Then all you have to do is study your scores, conduct performances, and enjoy the scenery. Let it be so!

The Extracurricular Program: Exercises

1. Choose a show and do a character study of all the main characters. Evaluate vocal range, musical style necessary for the role, dramatic qualities necessary, and dramatic or vocal "tricks" necessary (accents or physical deformities, to name two).

2. Pick five shows and discuss their suitability for presentation to the community you serve. What could be done to the script or score to make it more desirable?

3. Choose one composer of music for the musical theater. Tell why you believe him or her to be a good composer for this medium.

6

Non-Choral Concepts to Be Considered by a Choir Director

A. Preparing a Budget

There are many different ways in which school budgets are determined. The least satisfactory in terms of practicality and convenience to the teacher is the situation in which no set budget figure for the year is established. When the teacher has a need in his or her classroom, a request for funds is made to an administrator, and money may or may not become available from a general fund. The school's budgetary official makes a judgment call as to whether the request will be granted. This is an uncomfortable system, to say the least. It makes more sense for decisions regarding new purchases to be made by the person who perceives the need. Advanced planning is difficult when this budgetary practice is in effect. *The one situation in which this system is necessary and effective is to control the teacher who "needs" everything.*

A system that is one step better than the one described above also involves making requests through a general fund; however, there is one major difference from the first. A specific dollar figure within the general fund is established for each department in advance of the school year's opening, and the teacher is the administrator of those funds. It is the responsibility of the choir director to plan choral-related purchases for the entire year to accommodate all needs. The amount of money allotted for each curricular and co-curricular area within the school's overall program may be determined in several ways. A financial officer may study the all-school budget and dole out money to the various areas based on past years' purchases. He or she may have expertise in managing budgets and make decisions based on all-school needs and his own intuition. It is possible that the teacher will be consulted to establish a dollar figure for the year. The administrator who chooses this collegial approach is wise on two counts: 1) a more accurate picture of departmental needs will be projected, and 2) the teacher will feel that his or her input is necessary and valued. *A little boost to the self-esteem is never a bad thing.* This process of collecting information from the teacher must be done during the winter and spring of the year preceding the budget year, so it is necessary for all to plan in advance.

Another method for determining the funds for a given department (the one I believe is the most effective) lets the teacher submit a fairly detailed set of budget requests well in advance of the next school year. These itemized budgets are submitted to the financial officer and an all-school budget is set up based on the needs of each department. This system demands a lot of advanced planning on the part of every teacher.

The common thread in all of these budget methods is advanced planning. The days of simply spending any time a teacher had a "want" are over, if they ever existed. Purchases that must be made for April have to be projected a year earlier. Of course, unexpected needs will arise, and a process will be in effect that takes those requests into consideration. Following is an outline that may be of use in establishing a yearly budget. There will undoubtedly be as many variations of this format as there are school systems, but the general structure may be of some help, especially to a novice budget planner.

Supplies: The supplies request is the one that is probably the most important to the classroom teacher. Printed music is purchased with these funds; rentals, minor equipment items, and similar expenditures will be a part of this allotment. A useful rule of thumb is that any item that has a brief life expectancy should be considered part of the Supplies budget.

Maintenance and Repair: The monies allotted to this area are for upkeep of the department's equipment. There are at least three main areas to consider when establishing a figure for the Maintenance and Repair budget. One is cleaning and repairing costumes and uniforms owned by the department: Tuxedoes, robes, gowns, band uniforms are all to be considered. A second area is the upkeep of school-owned equipment—for instance, a riser needs repair or an equipment cart needs to be overhauled. Finally the upkeep of the department's musical instruments must be considered. To the choral director this means mainly the department pianos and any equipment owned for accompanying an ensemble or used in the pit for shows. How many piano tunings are necessary throughout the school year? What repair and overhaul needs are present? And don't forget synthesizers and other equipment used in general music and theory classes.

Equipment: This budget is used to purchase items which have a longer lifespan than those purchased in the Supplies budget. Requests for musical instruments (pianos and instruments used to accompany the choirs, as well as orchestra and band instruments) fall into this Equipment account. Large items such as risers and choral shells also come under this heading. It is important that in this category all purchases be prioritized since a lot of money is at stake. When a dollar figure is assigned, deciding which items to purchase is a matter of going down the list.

Library Purchases: In some schools, each department maintains a library, housed inside the music department, in addition to an all-school facility. Purchases for both areas are requested here. How many CDs will be needed to teach Music Appreciation next year? What books—recent or standard—should be added to the library holdings? Are there enough miniature scores to use in the Theory class? All of these are questions that find their answers in the Library budget.

Travel: The allotment of travel funds for attending conventions and workshops is, unfortunately, quickly becoming a thing of the past. If a school provides such funding, this is the budget used to request those monies.

Technology: As the twenty-first century unfolds, this will become more and more important in budget planning. The purchase of both hardware and software is considered here. Acquiring MIDI units falls into this category, as does the purchase of sound systems and recording equipment. And it is certain that there will be requests not even imagined today as the development of music technology continues.

All of the verbiage above constitutes merely an outline. Each school system's structure will be as different as each choir director's needs. I have included the budget template I have used for the past several years in Appendix E. Although I never did my departmental budget by any method other than pen and pencil, I feel sure there is now wonderful budget software available which will make this a much simpler task.

Just hope that you have a budget that is adequate for running your program, and that you don't have to sell candy to buy copies of "The Battle Hymn of the Republic."

B. Preparing a Student for College Music Study

The great majority of the students we see on a daily basis will take part in musical activities of some sort for the rest of their lives. They may continue to perform, taking advantage of the many musical activities available in the community: church choirs; community bands, orchestras, and choirs; and community theater, to name but a few. They may also choose to continue their involvement in music by being active and intelligent listeners, lending their support to those who perform. Participation at this avocational level will satisfy the needs of almost all of our students.

Then there is that small group of musicians who choose to involve themselves in music vocationally rather than avocationally. It falls to the music teacher to become both college counselor and career counselor for these students. Chances are very good that neither their parents nor the school's guidance counselors are prepared to provide the information necessary for entrance into these specialized music programs. (Upon re-reading that statement, I am aware that there are a few—a precious few—guidance counselors who are trained to counsel a potential music major. Consider yourself blessed if one is in your school.)

The information that follows is probably well known to you; after all, you have gone through all of this recently. I have included this information because there may be a few ideas in here which are new to you, and it may help to have all of this information down in black and white when you are counseling one of your students. I know that each of us comes from a different place with regard to what our students want and what our schools provide, but I believe that most of what I am writing will be applicable in many situations.

The first thing you and your student must discuss is the state of the student's performing ability—which is unfortunate, because it is not necessarily a valid indicator of success in many music fields. Almost all college music departments require an audition on the principal performing medium of the young performer. A student hoping to pursue a career in any of the various music fields must be ready to have his or her preparedness as a performer tested and evaluated as an important (the most important?) basis for admission to a college music program.

That is not to say that a student with less than brilliant performing skills should not consider a music career. Finding an appropriate school for each student becomes one of the first tasks for the guidance counselor, music teacher, student, and parents. Questions which must be asked and answered by the student and his or her family are legion. Here are a few.

How much money can the student's family afford?
How far away from home is appropriate for the student?
Does the student want a large- or small-school environment?
Given the size, geographic area, and financial requirements of the school, what are the student's financial aid necessities?
How difficult is it to be admitted to the schools of interest?
How high must the student score on standardized tests?
What GPA is necessary for admission? (Usually a seven-semester GPA.)

In these deliberations, high school guidance counselors can provide invaluable aid. They may have a computerized or online system for crunching this information and providing a list of possibilities. They undoubtedly know or can easily find out the level of test scores and cumulative average necessary for admission, and they can provide the necessary logistical information for each school in which the student is interested.

The process described above should take place during the junior year or the first semester of the senior year. When it is completed and the student and family have found several schools that seem to match the student's goals, the entire process changes hands to the student. Only he or she can prepare applications and auditions for admission.

Vocal performance may have different names in different university catalogs; by any name, it is the curriculum that is designed to prepare a student to become a professional performer. At the risk of offending many in the university music community, I will add that many feel that this degree, especially at the undergraduate level, is basically useless. Completing a vocal performance program at any school prepares a student to teach privately, which can be done without a degree; it prepares a student to sing professionally, which can be done without a degree; and it prepares a student to begin graduate study in music, which may be one road to becoming a college faculty member. There will, however, be those students who insist that a degree in performance is their only goal. Preparing an outstanding audition and choosing appropriate schools are the goals for these students. Make sure the student writes or calls the schools in question to get specific directions as to the preparation of an audition. How many songs? Of what type/style? Audition in person or by tape? (Chances of being admitted are much better in a live audition, not because the listeners are biased, but because recording techniques usually lead to a less brilliant offering than one performed live.) Will an accompanist be provided? These are just a few of the many questions which should be asked. Hopefully any student considering a performance degree will have a private teacher to prepare the student for this audition; if not, it becomes the classroom teacher's responsibility to make sure the audition is well prepared. All audition material should be memorized and *original* copies of the music provided for the accompanist. Do not ask to sing to a taped accompaniment, and never provide any professional with photocopied music.

Music education is the degree many students who don't want a career in performance choose to pursue. There are a number of reasons for this, and the chances are very good that the reader of this information can enumerate them very adequately, since that reader probably has, or is working toward, a degree in music education. There is a perception that a lower level of performing talent is necessary, that the colleges have different standards of excellence for music ed. students than they do for vocal performance majors. This may be true. I have never been a part of a committee to evaluate incoming students. Regardless, music education offers a degree that a graduate can use. Having finished the degree program often titled BME, a student can teach in the public schools. If he or she decides to pursue a performance major, the transition can be very smooth, since preparation in the major field will have been basically the same for both degree programs.

Having decided on a music education program of study, a student will need to prepare an audition (get particulars from the college), and possibly be prepared for a personal interview with a member of the music education faculty. He or she should probably be prepared to take tests in music theory and, possibly, music history. These written examinations are usually used for placement purposes rather than as admissions instruments. The student, the family, the private teacher, and guidance personnel all work with the classroom teacher to prepare the student for admission.

Music therapy, while not a new field, seems to be experiencing a renaissance of sorts. Students who believe that music therapy might be their goal will have to concentrate heavily on their choice of schools. A lot of schools offer no program in therapy; some offer a program of classroom instruction with little or no clinical experience; and precious few offer a program which includes classroom instruction, clinical experience, and medical school therapy classes. A student should have all three types of experiences before graduation. An internship, similar to student teaching for the education major, may be required. There is little standardization of graduation requirements from school to school, and there is similarly little standardization of certification from state to state. The student who is interested in getting a degree in music therapy has some homework to do regarding these differences before he or she chooses a college.

Once a student interested in music therapy has chosen a school that fits all the personal and family criteria as well as the professional criteria, it is then necessary to find out what the requirements are for an audition/interview. One school may apply a less stringent set of standards to the therapy candidate's performance audition. Another might expect the same level of expertise for all areas of study. Still another may require no performance audition at all. The student, with help from the guidance staff at his or her school, is responsible for retrieving the necessary information. If not actually required for entrance, competence on guitar and piano will certainly be graduation requirements.

Music industry degrees, such as recording engineering and music retailing, are probably the least standardized of all music-related degrees. In some schools very specific curricula leading to well-defined degrees are offered. At the other end of the spectrum are the schools in which the student designs his or her own curriculum to prepare for these types of careers. In some universities a music retailing program may be offered in the School of Business, with music courses required for successful completion of the degree program; in others, the School of Music offers the degree, and business courses are added to an existing curriculum. The same is true with recording engineering, but to a lesser extent. Because of the solidly musical nature of the goals of the recording profession, and because the technology of recording has become such an integral part of the music world, more work is usually offered in the music department. The guidance counselor may be of the most assistance in planning for degrees such as these.

After selecting a school, the student needs to carefully investigate entrance requirements. Depending on the structure of the program and in what department it is offered, a performing audition may not be required at all. Some schools require submission of a portfolio containing samples of the student's work for admission to a technologically oriented degree program such as recording engineering. Since all of these are specialized degrees, it is likely that the student and family will not have the range of choices of schools available to them that might be available to one seeking a more standard area of study. It will be necessary to go where the degree is offered.

Another course of study which involves instruction in two areas is *musical theater*. A few schools around the country have created a curriculum which combines studies in both the music and the drama departments, and the degree is confirmed by the Department of Musical Theater. A more common model is one in which the student is enrolled in one of the two departments, and the other department becomes a less-respected stepchild. Visiting various schools, talking to students enrolled in the programs, and studying the course catalogs will help inform the student as to the health of the program. The counseling staff at the high school may provide invaluable information, about this and other music degrees, that is available to them on the Internet.

The performance audition for an integrated musical theater program is very rigorous, involving singing, dancing, and acting. Preparation for this audition is hard work. The advice and guidance of coaches in all three areas is absolutely essential.

There are very few excellent musical theater programs. Choose wisely.

For all students who choose to pursue music as a career there is much preparation and a lot of personal homework to be done in advance of the audition. Preparation for college entrance in any of the music-related fields is a joint effort involving parents, classroom teachers, private teachers, counseling staff, and the student.

A suggestion: Begin right now preparing a college center in the music department. Order catalogs and audition information brochures from as many schools as seems practical. Keep them current. The college counselor in your school will be a terrific help in establishing your information center. This center will prove to be a very useful resource for the student considering advanced work in music.

C. Music Professional Organizations

They are great.
Join them.

Be active.

That may appear flippant, but it does describe my feelings very well. I believe that one of the most important things a teacher can do to keep his or her skills up to snuff, to keep abreast of the newest developments in technology and methodology, and to learn literature is to be active in these organizations.

Although by no means an exhaustive list, some of the professional organizations a choral director may be interested in joining are discussed below. Of course, the granddaddy of music organizations is the MENC: The National Association for Music Education, and its various state organizations. The biennial national conventions are full of learning sessions, wonderful performances, enlightening research reports, and plenty of time set aside for old friends to meet. In addition to these activities, which serve all that attend, there are business meetings and leadership sessions especially for officers and committee heads.

If you can't make the national conventions, don't miss your state meetings. It is at these meetings that you get to know those who are the leaders of your discipline, and the state conference is designed a lot like the national in that learning sessions, leadership sessions, business meetings, and performances are the main activities of the day.

At the local level, membership introduces you to your peers in the area and gives you opportunities for personal growth. Usually there are informal get-togethers, small-group meetings, and district conventions where someone will run a workshop on conducting techniques or a guest "expert" will come in to talk about rehearsal techniques. And literature! Always lots of talk about who's doing what, and what works and what doesn't.

The foregoing information is true of basically all of the organizations devoted to choral musicians and their development. The ACDA, American Choral Directors Association, is certainly an organization that no high school choral director (or student) should miss out on. Literature, conducting technique, musical style, and performances galore are mainstays at conventions of all levels.

In addition to these two associations, the choral director may very well be interested in investigating membership in the AGO,

American Guild of Organists, especially if his or her main background is church music. The IAJE, International Association of Jazz Educators, is the largest of the various jazz organizations, and the one most interested in vocal jazz as well as standard instrumental jazz.

Relatively few will ever become national officers in these professional organizations, but attendance at these conventions and involvement in national convention activities (honors choirs, for instance) are tremendous growth activities. At a typical three-or-four-day ACDA or MENC convention, it is probable that you will hear a dozen or more tremendous choral organizations of all styles, voicings, and levels. You will have the opportunity to attend research sessions and sessions on topics ranging from A to Z. And there will be literally rooms full of exhibits where you can find the latest in literature, technology, and equipment. Hopefully time spent with old friends and shared over a wonderful meal are also a part of any convention-going experience.

So:

They are great!

Join them.

Be active.

D. Why Should Music Be in the High School Curriculum?

After a very wise young man read my entry on budget planning, he said to me, "Doc, I think this information is good, but why should we spend tax money on music programs in the first place?" My initial reaction, since this young man had gone through my program a number of years earlier, was that he surely knew what he had gained from participation in music. That's why it's in the curriculum. But as I pondered the question, I realized that he was right; I should include a brief justification of music in the schools.

Much as I did for chapter 2, I looked to some other educators for answers to the question, but this time by researching a number of papers distributed by MENC over the years, I found a gold mine of information collected on their website: http://www.menc.org/information/prek12/principl.html.

In an online article titled "Why Is Music Basic: The Value of Music Education" (http://www.childrensmusicworkshop.com/musicisbasic.html), author unlisted, the question was asked, "Why should music be a part of a basic curriculum?" A few of the responses:

1. Music contributes to the school and community environment (quality of life).
2. Music helps prepare students for a career and is an avocation.
3. Music makes the day more alive and interesting, which in turn leads to more learning.
4. Music combines behaviors to promote a higher order of thinking skills.
5. It provides a way to image and create, contribute to self-expression and creativity.
6. Music enriches life, it is a way to understand our cultural heritage as well as other past and present cultures. . . .
7. Performing, consuming and composing are satisfying and rewarding activities.
8. Music contributes to sensitivity. . . .
9. Music education provides for perceptual–motor development.
10. It encourages team-work and cohesiveness.
11. It fosters creativity and individuality.
12. Music education adds to the self-worth of participants.
13. Music education fosters discipline and commitment.
14. It is a major source of joy and achievement.
15. Music provides unique and distinct modes of learning. . . .
16. Music is a therapeutic outlet for human beings.
17. It is a predictor of life's success. . . .
18. It develops intelligence in other areas. . . .
19. To provide success for some students who have difficulty with other aspects of the school curriculum.
20. To help the student realize that not every aspect of life is quantifiable and that it is important to cope with the subjective.
21. The music program is very cost-effective. . . .

Having read these statements, and bringing to mind President Reagan's statement (quoted in "Why Is Music Basic") to the effect that every man should be educated so he would be capable of restructuring civilization if it were ever destroyed, I discerned a very respectable cloak around our chosen discipline. If you are ever challenged, either in-school or out, refer to your own experiences and the literature of our professional organizations to draw up your own position paper.

Non-Choral Concepts: Exercises

1. Your job is at a high school of four hundred students, grades 9–12. Eighty of these students are in choral music, which meets daily. Your bosses expect a normal concert series (three or four concerts per year), and they will request entertainment at functions throughout the year. As you begin the school year, you go to a meeting with the financial advisor for the district, and he tells you that you have $700 to spend during the nine months ahead.

   Create a departmental structure, then begin to develop a budget for that department. You may assume that you have two pianos in good working order, if not of the finest quality. You are welcome to go into the files to provide some of the music for your concerts, and fundraising to supplement your budget is approved.

   Prepare a written budget to give to the administrator in charge of finances. Use a format which is *similar to* the one shown in Appendix E.

2. Jamie is a very good lower-voiced singer. Given the right training, she may very well turn out to be a fine *mezzo*. She has expressed an interest in continuing music study in college. She has done a little groundwork, and she thinks that she might be interested in teaching public school. You take it from there.

3. Four professional organizations were mentioned in this chapter. Look up each one and make a list of all the addresses, phone numbers, e-mail addresses, yearly dues, and the names of their national publications.

4. During the course of your teaching career you will be asked to draw up a number of position papers on various topics and for various audiences. The principal may need a position paper on why you are permitting songs with sacred texts to be sung for

presentation to the school board. The superintendent may want a position paper drawn up addressing your feelings about not rewriting a script for a musical. And it is very possible that they or the press may ask for a justification of your program and its place in the curriculum.

Start a collection of position papers today by writing one which explains the necessity of music, particularly choral music, in the high school curriculum. Use any information given above, and also check the ACDA Web site.

7

FIFTY THINGS NO ONE EVER TOLD ME

1. The times when there are the most job vacancies are late spring and late summer. Everyone would like to have a contract signed and plans made by May so they can kick back and enjoy the summer. The simple fact is that MANY jobs are not announced and filled until the week before school starts. Don't panic.
2. Faculty dress codes are not considered archaic in many schools. There may very well be a dress code for teachers. Find out before you sign a contract, and if it is a big enough concern for you, don't sign the contract.
3. Evaluating and negotiating the initial contract is the responsibility of the teacher. Before you sign any contract anywhere, ask questions about the following:

    Salary
    Benefits
    Sick leave
    Professional leave
    Emergency/personal leave
    Insurance (medical, dental, life, disability)
    Continuing education requirements and reimbursement
    Allotment for professional organization dues
    Maternity/paternity leave
    Expectations on your time beyond the school day
    Extra duty pay (this is a biggie for musicians)

    These are only the tip of the iceberg. Plan before you go into an interview and don't let yourself be hurried.
4. Believe it or not, retirement will be here soon. Save as if it were beginning tomorrow.

5. When you leave one job to take another or to go back to school, do *not* take the money you have put into your retirement account out of that fund to use in your new venture. Personal insight: I retired this year; it has taken me seven years' worth of healthy payments to buy those five years of service back into my portfolio. You will need those credits and that money.

6. Paying Uncle Sam requires a major part of the paycheck. Way too much of your check goes back to the government, but there is little you can do about it. Set up a meeting soon after employment with the district payroll manager. He or she can give you the figures you don't want to see, and will know some legal ways you can increase the size of your refund in the spring.

7. There is a formula established which determines the amount of money you will receive upon retirement. Retirement benefits are figured differently from state to state. In many, Social Security is your retirement plan and you can get information at any time during your employment by contacting your local Social Security office. In some, a state teachers' retirement system controls the benefits, and different formulas for figuring your retirement pay are in effect. Generally, you will receive an amount based on the number of years you have taught, the salary you have received, and the amount you have invested in the system.

8. The rules about giving private lessons to students for money vary from place to place. Giving them for free is always OK. Just make sure you know the rules in advance. If you cross a certain line, you are guilty of "double dipping," collecting both tax money and personal money for teaching a student on school time.

9. Begin a tax sheltered annuity or similar savings plan with your very first check. Do not skip a payment, even if it is only one dollar that you can afford to save. Each month, on that day you write checks, pay yourself first, regardless of other bills. Only when you do that will you really be committed to a program of saving for the future.

10. Becoming a union member may be required, and it can be expensive. What do you think about the National Education Association? About local bargaining units? About unions? These

questions have to be answered before you worry about paying dues. In a short statement, the dues can be expensive; have the money withdrawn a little at a time from your paycheck.

11. Money may be available from your school to aid with convention-going expenses. Money for convention attendance is on the decline. Fewer and fewer schools are paying for room, board, and transportation. Ask for the moon, but chances are good you will get only a little stardust, if anything.

12. There is usually district money available to hire a clinician (guest conductor, institute day speaker). It's true, but you may have to do some bush-beating to find it.

13. Make sure you take courses in the use of a music printing program before you start your new assignment. It is entirely possible that you will need to teach students how to use it the second day you are employed. In theory classes, in laboratory classes and open labs, *Finale* and many of its look-alikes are taught before any work is done in the class. Students with free time may want to write out a song they have written by ear. Advanced instrumentalists and vocalists may want to put an arrangement on paper. The uses of these programs in the department are virtually endless. You must know how to run them and how to troubleshoot their idiosyncrasies.

14. The two most important people for you to know are the principal's secretary and the head of the maintenance department. Keep them on your side. These two folks control what gets done in a school building.

15. To assure yourself of good service, slip a six-pack or some cookies to those who render you good service, and whose goodwill you need to cultivate—the janitor in your department, the printer, helpful secretaries, and others. These people often do the most and hardest work in the building, and they are seldom even thanked. Cookies, beer, or other goodies are minor investments on your part, and they will yield results.

16. Make friends with the coaching staff—male and female. A bit tongue-in-cheek; however, the job of recruiting singers at the high school level is a never-ending task, and being a solid friend of the athletic program will make that job a lot easier.

17. Meet and make friends with your musical counterparts in the area. Meet all the other choir directors within your township. When you do a combined concert or run into one of these peers, it is good if you know the conductor's name. These people can give you a lot of insight about your administration, about community expectations and boundaries.

18. No matter how much money is in the budget, you always need $3,000 more. This statement is another way of saying that you will never have all the money you want, either in your salary or in your department budget. Learn to separate "need" from "want."

19. The powers-that-be may not share the choral director's concern over the condition of the departmental piano(s). If you have a piano that is a piece of junk, and you'd like to get rid of it and buy a new one but your administration says "no," simply make sure it is used at every PTA meeting, school board reception, and public presentation you give. Others will notice. Having said that, I am aware that I would never actually do it because it would compromise the quality of the performance aspect of the department. I guess I would bite the bullet and just keep working on whoever controls the purse strings.

20. The acoustics in the choir room may be unacceptable. Assuming that you have the support of your district for the funds, get in touch with a representative of the company you have chosen to provide the large equipment for your choral program (risers, choral shells); they can draw up a plan of acoustical treatment for your room—free. Of course, they will expect the opportunity to make a pitch when it comes to purchase time.

    If you don't have any money available to you, do what you are capable of doing yourself. Hang curtains; put acoustic tile on walls and/or ceilings; create false walls using departmental equipment such as shells, risers, and pianos.

21. It is the choir director's responsibility to know where to buy the equipment necessary for a choral program—risers, shells, and pianos, to name a few. The same is true for instrumentalists, but to a much greater degree. While I am not the slightest bit shy about writing what I think of philosophies and methods, I

won't give a retail endorsement in this forum. The place for you to make these decisions is at music conventions. One of the highlights of most conventions is the exhibits area, where manufacturers and their representatives show off their product lines. It won't take you too many visits to the exhibits area before you can make decisions about choral music products. (Also, if you work it right you can save lunch money by visiting the booths that give away their fundraising products.)

22. No matter how many computers you need for a music theory project, there will be two fewer than that number available to you in good working condition. As technology becomes more and more prevalent, the problem of too little hardware for a class will disappear. Start gently nudging the appropriate people in your school toward the building of a MIDI lab in your department. It will happen. In the meantime, set up a schedule for using what you have, including before and after school and lunch periods.

23. A lot of administrators dictate what should be included in a choir program. It is best to find out in advance what the administrators of your school want in terms of public presentation. Usually, specific requests will be few, but be prepared to act on them immediately. Unfortunately, my advice is the same if a "request" comes right out of left field. Do it today. You can begin an informal program of educating your audiences and your bosses little by little at a later date. Secure your job first.

24. Your immediate supervisor, your boss, may be a non-musician. You are directly responsible to someone—either a fellow musician who serves as department chair or instructional supervisor, or possibly a front-office administrator. In either case, respect their advice and take their suggestions. As long as you are doing your job there is no reason to fear this person. When you receive suggestions from that person, follow them. He or she has no stake in your career; help is being offered; take it.

A hint to ease anxiety when you are being evaluated: look at your audience and picture that evaluator in his or her night clothes or underwear; you will find your fear of that person is greatly diminished.

25. Choose your battles wisely. Over the years of your career, you will have a lot of complaints about the people around you, about your bosses, about policies. Pick the important ones over which you choose to do battle and learn ways to ignore or live with the rest. When something major comes up, fight to the end; the end comes when the top person in the food chain makes a decision. Then you must live with the decision. Sometimes you will win; sometimes you will lose. When you win, be gracious, and when you lose, act gracious.

26. There is a giant educational pendulum that swings back and forth, bringing with it old ideas, methods, and concepts in the guise of new ideas. What you are learning in your methods classes today will be old hat in ten years; it will return, with a new name, in twenty.

27. Some administrators are the first to embrace these "new" ideas.

28. The performance of sacred music in a high school setting is often a point for discussion. Religion has, for centuries, been the breeding ground for choral music composition. Much of the music in our music libraries is sacred in nature. If for no reason other than the great amount of sacred literature available, the choral music of our various religious heritages should play a major role in our choral programs.

   It is my personal opinion that one should strive to achieve a balance among the sacred texts of the several cultures represented in the student body of the school. If a school has a significant Jewish population, make sure Jewish literature is represented in concerts—and not the "Dreidel Song." You will have to look HARD to find quality Jewish choral literature, but it does exist. Try calling your local synagogue's cantor. For other religious and ethnic groups' music, go to the source and ask questions. After saying this, I should add that I still feel free to perform music with Christian texts since the schools in which I have taught have been mainly peopled by nominal Christians.

   Two excellent publications on this subject are available from MENC. One is titled "Music with a Sacred Text," and the other is called "Religious Music in Our Schools." These are available to you in multiples from MENC (1806 Robert Fuller Drive, Reston, Virginia, 20191).

29. The choice of a costume is a major issue for parents and administration as well as performers. Within your program it really doesn't matter as long as what you choose is in good taste, is matching throughout the ensemble, and is neat and clean. Make your choice any way you like. Kids (especially those of the feminine persuasion) will never like what you choose. You will probably need a set of robes for multi-school performances.

30. A choir that looks bad almost always sounds bad.

31. Sometimes fundraising is necessary to keep the music program afloat. Unfortunately, fundraising will probably be a necessity at some point in your program. Taxes can only underwrite so much of a school's expenses. You may have to sell wrapping paper to buy new robes or to pay for extracurricular activities and the like. If you find yourself in a situation where you have to raise funds to buy music for your classes, find a new job.

    FYI: Those same convention exhibits that have products displayed will have representatives from fundraising companies present. Look over their products; find out your margin of profit. Another idea source is the mailings you will receive constantly; check with the Student Activities Office for mailings, as well.

32. Prepare folders in advance of the first rehearsal. A lot of people hand out music each day, or lay the music on the piano for singers to pick up at the beginning of rehearsal. The singer needs to be able to mark his or her own music and review those marks each rehearsal.

33. Keep all of your music cataloged, if for no other reason than that you should be able to lay your hands on any piece of music in your library very quickly. But more importantly, we are stewards of the school's assets.

34. Keep a close accounting of all music in student folders. At the cost of music today, you can't afford to lose even one copy. It now costs over $2.00 to replace an octavo that cost $0.80 per copy only a few years ago. In Appendix B I have given you the

library system used at the school where I taught; it's a home-made system that works. There are also several really excellent library systems that can be purchased commercially. And for the more computer literate among us, there are a ton of comput-erized library programs. It's not important how you catalog and keep track of your music, just make sure it is done. Students can be a great help.

35. Copying music *for any reason* without permission is against the law. Enough said.

36. The industry and our professional organizations have provided us with material with which we can gain permission to copy in some cases. MENC provides a form you can use to ask a pub-lisher's permission to copy a piece of music that is permanently or temporarily out of print. Write to them and ask for appro-priate forms, and then use them. Make sure you keep copies of the completed forms in the music file.

37. ACDA publishes a Request for Permission to Arrange form which should be used any time you make an arrangement of copyrighted material for your choirs. It is no mistake that this and the previous statement require the same mantra: The in-dustry and our professional organizations have provided us with material with which we can gain permission to copy in some cases. Write to them and ask for the appropriate forms, and then use them. Make sure you keep copies of the completed forms in the music file.

38. Regardless of your background and training, you may be "asked" to mount a full-scale musical—in an auditorium, or a gym, or a cafeteria. For some young teachers, this looks like an impossible task. It's not. There is no question that those who have done some stage work before they are "asked" to direct the musical will have an easier time of it than those who have not, but the solution to the problem of mounting any produc-tion in any space is to get help. Take a look at the section of this book dealing with presenting a musical. It may answer a lot of your questions.

My second suggestion is to you personally. Get out there

and PERFORM. There is no substitute for first-hand experience. Community theater is a great outlet. Try out for a summer stock job. If you are not selected to be in the cast, get down and dirty by building sets, painting sets, and pulling ropes. Do anything to learn.

39. It may not be OK for Bloody Mary to say "stingy bastard." In other words, should you rewrite a script so that it does not offend the majority of your audience? You can receive a lot of good advice from your administration, but my immediate reaction is "no." Don't do it. A fine writer produced the script in your hands. If you can't perform the script as written, choose another show. It is that black and white in my mind.

    An aside: It is getting harder and harder to find shows that can be produced as written, even in a fairly liberal community. Plots that may be unsuitable for teenagers (*Company*), language that is objectionable to many (*Rent*), and vocal lines which are too demanding for most young voices (*Evita*) are becoming more apparent. My black and white has had to admit a little bit of gray in the past couple of years.

40. You'd better skip the cast party after the musical. If there is even a one-in-a-million chance that a student will bring Jack Daniels to the party, your presence makes the party a school-sponsored activity (if not legally, certainly in people's eyes). You can let your kids know how much you appreciate their work in other ways.

41. No matter how good a given performance is, there will be those in the audience who will offer "positive criticism." Some people find fault in the most beautiful of efforts; somehow it makes them taller when they can cause someone else to appear shorter. Ignore them completely; it was their ancestors who said that da Vinci had no sense of color.

42. No matter how bad a performance is, there will always be one audience member who comes up afterwards to tell you that your show was "better than Broadway." Those compliments always sound so great at the time, but don't put too much stock in them. Some people tend to confuse their pride in the students

they are watching with the excellence they saw in New York. But revel in the compliment and REPEAT IT TO ALL THE PERFORMERS.

43. Morale among staff members dips when excellence is not rewarded. A simple note from the principal saying that your spring concert was enjoyable and sending congratulations to all of the performers is all it takes to create a feeling of goodwill.

44. Supervising a student teacher is hard work when done correctly. A corollary is this: Don't expect a student teacher to lighten your load during a particularly heavy semester. Student teachers come in two varieties: good and bad. With good student teachers you will need to clear some time in your schedule to give them the enrichment they need to achieve excellence in their work. These student teachers will bring new life to your program, and you will need to spend a lot of time observing them to see where to go with them.

On the other hand, a really poor student teacher demands a lot of your time to help him or her identify the problems in their teaching. The two of you may never reach the most elementary stage of music preparation. For many, the ability to identify and try to correct problems may be the ultimate goal of student teaching.

Once in a great while, a student teacher will arrive who just is not cut out to be a teacher. They may write great lesson plans, but they can't carry them out. They lack that certain indefinable something that is necessary to become a good teacher. When you are assigned a student teacher who fits into this category, call his or her school immediately. Set up a meeting with the coordinating teacher and at least one Music Education faculty member. Share your concerns about the student. Make whatever recommendations you feel are in order. Some of the schools you work with will listen to your suggestions; others will not. You need to spend the rest of your time together leading the young person to a thoughtful consideration of future career goals.

45. Finding accompanists who are competent is a difficult task. First of all, look for a student accompanist. A shy person may

not assert him or herself to volunteer; a singer may not want to play in lieu of singing. Then make a concerted effort among the parents of the singers. There are a lot of moms and dads who have the time free but have never considered volunteering. Ask them. If all comes to naught, hit your administration up for funds to hire someone in the musical community to do the job.

46. Don't ever touch student monies. The students have just completed a candy sale to buy new shoes for performance. You collect all the money and keep it in a lockbox in your office. The next day, when you count it, you come up $370 short. You know that you didn't take it, and your students probably know that you wouldn't take it. But you have left yourself wide open for someone—a parent, a disgruntled student, a community member who just likes to stir up trouble—to accuse you of theft. Proof isn't necessary to end your effectiveness as a teacher, only the accusation.

47. Regardless of the amount of insurance you have on your car, do not give students rides in it. The world is different today than when many of us started teaching. It is no longer enough to refrain from evil; it is necessary to refrain from all appearance of evil as well.

48. Giving grades is a pain in the patoot, but most schools require it. Giving grades is a necessary evil in the public schools. I base a student's grade on three things:

1. attendance, at school and in concerts (A student who misses a concert will be assigned a hefty make-up task if a parental excuse is received within three days of the absence);
2. part-learning, as evidenced by performing in quartets, trios, etc., in front of the choir; and
3. quiz and test grades gathered over the marking period. These quizzes and tests relate to the acquisition of basic musical skills. Try to make lemonade out of the lemons of grade assignment. Use the giving of grades as part of the students' learning experience in choir.

49. It is absolutely essential that you keep your gradebook in tip-top shape with all assignments, absences, and test and quiz scores noted. A gradebook is considered to be a legal document. Schools keep gradebooks either in their original form or on microfiche or stored in some other format. Colleges are sometimes interested in a grade several years after a student has graduated. Auto insurance discounts are given on the basis of high school grades in many cases. Someone may contest a grade several years after a student graduates. Make sure everything is in the book.

50. Expect to spend a minimum of ten hours at school each day. "Most teachers work from sun to sun. The music teacher's work is never done." We joke about it; we complain about it; but it is a fact. And many days are longer than that by the time we teach all day, have a rehearsal after school, run out to get a bite to eat, and direct a couple of evening rehearsals.

    The youngest among us are usually the most driven, and they tend to work the longest hours. (I am fully aware that we all know many exceptions to that statement. I stand by it.) Make sure that while you are living this hectic life, your family is somehow invested in it as well. If not, you may find that understanding at home wears thin. Look around you at the next district festival and count the number of divorced band and choir directors.

    Don't lose sight of the important things in life as you build that wonderful instrumental or vocal program. It really isn't all that important that you do forty community appearances at Christmas time. It's probably much more important for those students to have some time to share the holidays with their families, and your family would probably enjoy spending some holiday time with you as well.

EPILOGUE: FROM OTHER VANTAGE POINTS

"From Other Vantage Points" is provided as an answer to a concern that the book is limited in scope to schools of a particular size and socioeconomic level. This is a concern I don't refute in the slightest; I can only write about what I know, and I know about large middle-class, suburban high schools.

To attempt to fill the noted chasm, I interviewed seven directors of high school choral music programs. The subjects of the chapters of my book were given to them and they were asked to give input on each, as it applies to their teaching situation. The seven respondents represented the following types of schools:

Large suburban
Upper class
Small, rural
Heavily multicultural
Mostly African-American, middle class
Large urban (not inner-city)
Suburban school, disadvantaged (in an effort to stay very positive, I may have identified this school according to different descriptors)

The information gained from this additional information is useful, I believe. It gives very important alternatives to the information I share, and in many ways supports the information originally given. The most interesting thing to me was seeing how the men and women tailored these basic choral concepts to fit their situations and their students.

A. Getting Started

1. Building a Choral Program

First Respondent: That depends upon the resources available. If it's possible to set up your young voices so that boys are together and girls are together, that's the thing to do. I think the thing to do is to have three groups: a boys' chorus, a girls' chorus, and a mixed chorus.

Second: I rather like the set-up I work with now, so I would try as much as possible to replicate it. I would have a freshman girls' chorus. The next group up would be sophomore girls and freshman and sophomore boys, the next group up would be mainly junior girls and some seniors, and the top group would be a mixed group of juniors and seniors. We used to try to separate the freshman men into their own group, but enrollments weren't strong enough to justify that.

Third: I'm tied into one mixed choral group in my curriculum because of the size of the school. Beyond that, everything I do is on my own. I do have a boys' group and a girls' group, but they are not part of the curriculum. To place the students in that choir, I talk to them first. I ask them questions and try to ascertain their background. If they seem to have a strong musical background I go ahead and place them in the section where they are most comfortable. I do want to hear each student individually, but some are so nervous that I came up with the idea of having each student make a tape singing "Happy Birthday." That's something they all know, and they usually are OK with doing a tape. Then I use these tapes to place them and to compare their progress over the next several years, as they do a tape every semester.

Fourth: I would set up first a girls' choir and a boys' choir. I think it is absolutely crucial for the younger boys to be in a class by themselves. Then, depending on the number of students enrolled, I would start a "cadet" mixed chorus and, for lack of a better word, a concert choir. The concert choir would be my older and more mature students, and the mixed choir would be for the kids just past the youngest groups.

Fifth: An ideal program would be fairly free from stress—little or no competition—and would probably be composed of a boys' chorus, a girls' chorus, a swing choir, and a concert choir. In a school our size, the same group of kids do everything, so boys' chorus, girls' chorus, and swing choir meet before school, and concert choir is a part of the school day.

Sixth: Considering the prevailing trends in the area where I teach, I would probably begin with a show choir, possibly two, and then add training groups.

Seventh: The program I would establish would be ability-based, and the top of that program would be a mixed choir, preferably of older singers. I would separate the youngest singers into female and male ensembles. This makes it possible to spend more time on vocal development. I would also plan a chorus for the kids who do not want to perform, for those who just want to sing without the pressure of performance. In all groups we would sing music of many different styles. If I inherited a program which was already established, I would work toward that kind of program, but if I started from scratch I would start with a mixed group.

2. Choosing and Purchasing Music

First Respondent: First of all they should rely on the music they learned in high school and college. Then they should get involved in their professional groups to learn new literature and to meet local music merchants as well as big organizations like Kidder and Pepper. If possible, I would get on the mailing list of all the local and big jobbers; it's amazing how many things they have available to us now—like CDs.

Second: The first thing I would do is to call some of the other teachers in the area to find out where they get their music. I would also consider the big companies like J.D. Pepper, especially because they will send you single copies to look at. To choose music I would rely heavily on my collegiate and high school experiences with music. I would attend as many conventions and music reading workshops as I could find, and I would try a couple of brand new tunes so that I stayed challenged.

Third: I refer to my old background a lot; I go down into my basement and find things I like, some old chestnuts. In addition I may order three or four new numbers that I have heard at festivals or reading sessions. I *very rarely* go through the catalogs because they are full of what I call "pop poop." I'd much rather get copies of pop music from the Waring library at Penn State. It's available to everybody; just write to Pete Kiefer. It's free; he'll send it. When—if—I buy a new piece of music I usually go through Pepper because they have an 800 number and I can call from my office. Simplicity.

Fourth: I think I would find first a reputable dealer and talk to their choral expert and get his or her ideas about what will work for the kids in this community. When I taught, I would call a certain man and tell him, "I need some music for a beginning mixed chorus that is soprano-heavy," or whatever. Nine times out of ten he would send me a packet of music. I seldom even bothered with buying his suggestions "on approval." I trusted his judgment. Also, if I were familiar with the community, I would go around and just listen to other choirs. There was one man I pestered to death sitting in his choir rehearsals—of course I asked for permission first—and just soaking up everything that was going on. Including literature. I got some of my best ideas that way.

Fifth: We get a lot of our stuff initially on approval from J. W. Pepper. We use the required list for the state as a guideline. We can listen to the things on the computer, which makes it a lot easier to make decisions. And we use our college and high school backgrounds, which have familiarized us with a lot of literature.

Sixth: I go to my local music store and study new releases, and I use the demo discs and tapes sent from certain publishers.

Seventh: First of all, I would buy absolutely nothing until I had met the choirs and gotten a general idea of their levels. During that time period, we would sing songs the students are likely to know or should know, such as "The Star-Spangled Banner," "America," show tunes they are likely to have heard, and pop music with musical integrity. When I began to buy music, I would contact local music stores and major distributors (like Pepper). I would also make myself familiar with the repertoire they had sung in the past.

3. Before School Begins

First Respondent: I think I would try to talk to the previous choir director, if he or she is available, to find out the level of the program that preceded your coming . . . and to find out the administration's expectations of you and the program. Let's see . . . oh yes, I'd talk to the people at the junior high to find out what to expect.

Second: First of all, I would get into the existing music library, learn its contents, and evaluate its usefulness. I would pick a few works to begin immediately as soon as the kids arrive. If there were time, I think I'd try to have some sort of social activity at least with the top choir. We could have sort of a pre-school workshop. And I would bake cookies.

Fourth: I get copies of the music required for state competition and pick my music from that. Then I spend time over the summer studying that music and developing my goals, based on the content of those songs.

Fifth: The first thing I would do is to get in touch with another music teacher in the community to find out where the program was, so that I could get started right at the beginning at a level they are accustomed to. I would find out what kind of literature they had performed. I would talk to administrators about budget, about my schedule, find out if there was a hired accompanist or not. If one were available, I would definitely get in touch with him. Let's see, budget, schedule . . . oh, yes, uniforms. They can be a real pain in the butt. I'd also want to know if there was a booster organization or not, and if there was, I'd want to get hold of the leaders of that group. I guess those are a few of the things I can think of off the top of my head. In addition to that I think I would get a simple number out and ready to sing right from the beginning, so they know this is a class for singing.

Sixth: My first job would be to learn my music thoroughly. Then I would need to get a staff in place, at least a choreographer and a pianist.

Seventh: Each year I schedule a time to meet with administrators, especially counselors and the principal, to talk about the upcoming year for the choirs. In the earliest years I would want to find out as much as possible about the existing structure, how it met the needs of the school, and I would get information about enrollment figures. I would look for advice about recruitment procedures. I would prepare the song sheets we will sing from at the beginning of the year, and I would put together a packet of graphics to help me teach basic vocal technique. Also, I take a look at myself, wardrobe, physical look, those sorts of things. I want to be "looking good" when I first meet the singers.

B. Choral Basics in the Rehearsal

1. Warming Up the Choir

First Respondent: Warm-ups are, I think, essential, but I think it is important that you draw them from where they are. In other words, listen to the kids to learn what their vocal abilities are, what their vocal needs are, and then go from there as you warm them up. I would, as much as possible, take a daily warm-up from the music to be rehearsed that day.

Second: As you well know, I think warm-ups are the heart of the rehearsal. They can be used to work on tone, and that is my forte. I also use warm-ups for vowel unification and breathing. Toward the end of a typical warm-up period, I introduce exercises that are specifically related to problem areas in the music we will rehearse that day. I like to rehearse in ascending patterns, and I know that flies in the face of many other directors' practices. I don't talk much about registers because many students will invent a register problem in their voices as a result of introducing the concept. When a problem arises, solve it. Otherwise, don't cause it.

Third: Ah, warm-ups. It's working on pitch matching, tone production, vowels. I work with them on developing vibrato and in getting rid of it. I teach them the value of straight-tone singing, that vibrato tends to bring the pitch down. We talk a lot about pitch, about taking care to always sing in tune. We sing a lot of unison and octave tones; we glide around a lot—using chromatics, to tune up their ears. We do a lot of physical things, like sticking our fingers in front of our faces to feel for air. We do a lot of listening to other sections. We also warm up using concepts from the music in their folders. If we are going to rehearse something that is terribly high, we will work hard on the upper range. If there is a particularly difficult rhythmic phrase in one of the pieces, we will take that out of context and learn it.

Fifth: One of the things I do—I don't know, this may be a fairly unconventional answer—is to pick excerpts from the music in the folder and use them to warm up. I would find something in the music that I think is going to be problematic, and I work that in different keys, on the vowels of the words. I don't generally warm up just going up chromatically. I have learned that the kids catch on to that, so I don't always have their attention. So I jump around to different keys. In my opinion, all too often the warm-ups are not even related to what they are going to sing, and that is wasting time.

Sixth: Never skip a warm-up period, either physically or vocally. The muscles in the body and the voice need to be warmed up to prevent stress during both rehearsal and performance.

Seventh: I set aside about one fourth of every rehearsal for warm-ups. In this period I need to warm the choirs up in three areas—physically, mentally, and vocally. We do exercises to relax muscles and practice breathing. We vocalize to develop tone quality, extend range, and improve technique. I spend time with the guys developing falsetto and blending it *down* into the full voice. This helps the guys sing higher with a full tone quality. I think it is important to vary the warm-up period from day to day. I use different exercises, different vocalises, and I change the order I do things in. If it becomes time just to "live through" until the "real" rehearsal begins, it loses its purpose. I never skip this warm-up session.

2. *The Unison Sound*

First Respondent: I am very fond of using unison singing in the all-boys and all-girls groups especially because I don't have to deal with the discrepancy of the octave jump. It is a great tool for teaching pure, clear sounds, focus of tone, diction—all of these. And I think unison singing in a mixed choir is essential because of the varying colors it provides. And there, too, it is a tool to work on sound.

Second: I don't have unison singing as a high priority in my work. I do make a point of making sure students know when they encounter an area in a piece. Then we work on listening to balance sections and individuals.

Third: I use a lot of unison; it kind of exposes them. We listen for unison then take the time to tune it, listening to each other.

Fifth: I honestly feel, Walt, that if you can't sing in unison, there is no reason to go into parts, because I believe unison singing is harder. Generally the young teacher is not going to think unison is important. I work on unison in much the same way as I work on vowels, slow it down and sing very softly so you can hear each other. I have even been known to start with one singer and add on, one at a time. That's good; oh, watch the vowel sounds.

Sixth: Unison singing is very important in the show choir literature. It is easier to produce a good sound while dancing if the music is unison. But we work hard on a good sound and matching vowels and consonants.

Seventh: Unison singing is probably the most difficult thing I do with my choirs. Certainly it is not necessarily a challenge as far as notes are concerned, but to achieve the balanced sound that is necessary to create unison is a real challenge to me. First of all, all of the singers have to sing the exact pitch; an out-of-tune pitch will ruin the tonal balance of the piece. Secondly, vowels and diphthongs need to be identically formed and produced. If fifteen singers sing a nice, round *oo* vowel, but the sixteenth produces his or her *oo* sound with a lot of *ee* thrown in, any hope of unison vowel sound is out the window. And the same is true for dynamics, rhythm, and all the other musical elements in choral singing. As much as I personally do not appreciate the genre, if you want to hear really good unison singing, listen to a fine barbershop quartet.

3. Vowels, Diphthongs, and Consonants

First Respondent: Although I think the conductor must have a thorough knowledge of vowel formations, I don't think it is always necessary for the kids to get hung up on vowel production. The conductor can shape and mold vowels and consonants in the context of the warm-up period.

Second: This is a book in itself. I will give you what I think are the most important concepts associated with diction:

Consonants energize the singing.

Use pure vowels, and let the voice ring. Give it freedom. Don't introduce a bunch of rules which inhibit the sound.

Third: I tell them that the matching vowel, vertically, is what makes the difference between our high school choir and every other high school choir in the country. That's what I talk about. Yes, and then we practice "turning" the end because you can't sing pop music without using the diphthong. It depends a lot on the style of music. We talk a lot about voiced and unvoiced consonants.

Fifth: These are very important because as we know this is what we sing on: the color of the vowel, the shape of the vowel. This is, in my opinion, the most important thing I do in a rehearsal. I go about working on vowels by singing something slow and just sit on notes and work on the vowels. Uniformity of vowels is so often missing. Also, bring the volume way down so we can hear. I call it "singing with your ears." When it comes to consonants as well as diphthongs, I model a lot. I find that it helps if the kids know what it is I am looking for.

Sixth: After I have taught the so-called "pure" vowels and consonants, I find it necessary to spend a lot of time teaching how to modify them to achieve stylistic accuracy.

Seventh: Of course, the key to everything we sing is the vowel and consonant sounds we make. I spend a lot of time in every warm-up period working on vowel sounds. I start with the *oo* sound because it is the easiest for me to describe and ultimately teach to the kids. Once we have established that sound, it is relatively easy to move to the other vowels that are produced in that same mouth position: *oh, ah,* and their derivatives. Then we work on the vowels produced in the *ee* mouth position and their derivatives (*ee, ay, ih,* and *eh*). Then we spend time with the most often-used diphthongs—*ow, eye, ay,* and *you.* These are the sounds that allow us to create the various tone qualities in our singing, but, in my opinion, it is the consonants that create language out of these sounds, so I spend a lot of time drilling those sounds. I also think it is very important that both vowel and consonant sounds match the style of the music. An *ah* vowel in a Schubert mass is completely different than the *ah* sound in a pop number, like "Higher and Higher." Knowing and being able to produce these various sounds is the key to singing a text so that you're stylistically correct.

C. The Academics of the Rehearsal

1. Teaching Sight-Singing

First Respondent: Absolutely essential. My God, if you don't teach people to read music you aren't a teacher. There are a lot of "methods" of teaching sight-singing; I happen to prefer solfège. For a text I use the old Oliver Ditson *Melodia,* but it has limitations.

Second: SOLFÈGE! I use a book called *The Sol-Fa Book* (published by Dickson-Wheeler, Inc., Weems, Virginia) to introduce and drill solfège concepts. We write syllables in our music for everything we rehearse. I have found that pitch is much improved because they learn what *do* to *fa* sounds like, and it is easy to tune that every time. Once they have learned *ti* to *do* they have learned the concept of the leading tone, and then they sing it better in tune. The only problem we run into is transferring from solfège to lyrics.

Third: I'll just tell you what I do. I try to go about "demystifying" the art of reading music. We have to go back to learning that up the keyboard is up the scale; that going down in pitch is going down in notes on the staff. It's sad to have to do that, but a lot of my kids come in not knowing. We take something as simple as "Jingle Bells" and start on a pitch and ask them to draw that on the staff. I do Kodály, starting almost immediately. I'll take, say, *do* to *sol* on one day and ask them to watch me as I sign out a piece I have written on the board. Then I have them join me, and pretty soon they are doing it—with a great sense of accomplishment. I don't let anybody not take part. Pretty soon they have lost that fear of reading music, and they are making music.

Fifth: I'm fanatical about it; fanatical about it. I have a program that starts with single-line sight singing, because, generally speaking, singers don't have the slightest idea how to sight-sing. They are used to singing by rote. I use a movable *do,* and we begin with very easy examples — on solfège — always use solfège. I have all of this written out so that we have something to start with. The reason I had to do this is that I am not pleased with any of the published material. Usually they start out OK — some of them even start out wonderful — but by page five we're into graduate school. You know what I mean? They all move too fast. I learned a lot from the language arts teacher. "Move slowly and repeat, repeat, repeat." Remember when we were learning to read? It was, "See Spot. See Spot run. Run, Spot, run." Over and over and over. It's got to be the same thing with sight singing. Keep exercises short and diatonic. When the kids have success, they are more likely to go on. At first they don't want to practice sight-reading, but pretty soon they accept the fact that we're going to do it, and that's it. They just accept it. So, yes, I am fanatical about sight-singing.

Sixth: I don't spend a lot of time teaching sight-singing; we learn by reading a lot of literature.

Seventh: I teach sight-reading in my choirs religiously. Along with warm-ups, there is a specific time period set aside daily for learning and practicing the skill. I start with rhythm. Even with my oldest students we learn to identify and perform rhythmic patterns using the usually-more-early-childhood technique of *ti, te, tah,* and the others. Instituting this process allows me to put aside concepts like beats per measure and beats per note and lets us zero in on the relationship between notes, much the same way solfège functions with pitch. And that is the other step — solfège. With my background of private piano and voice lessons, I was never taught a system for sight-singing, and I find these are excellent approaches. I have never found a book that meets my choirs' sight-singing needs, so I make song sheets for each new lesson. As with warm-ups, I never completely miss a sight-reading lesson.

2. Acquiring Basic Skills in the Choral Classroom

First Respondent: They need to know letter names of notes in both clefs. They need to know tempo markings, articulation markings, dynamic markings. [Interviewer: How do you find the time?] You make time. At the beginning of the rehearsal, or even at the end, you set aside time to talk about and respond to topics you put on the board or bring up for discussion. Paired with this is, I believe, testing, written testing covering the technical aspects of the music: knowledge of key signatures and knowledge of time signatures, for instance. And this time does not take away from the choral part of the rehearsal; it adds to it.

Second: The choir rehearsal must be used for more than just preparing concerts. Many years ago, we developed a program of choral objectives. These objectives are divided into two types. On the one hand are a series of written objectives. These cover topics associated with theory, with terminology, scales, chords, and those sorts of things. The other type of objectives are singing objectives; these are tests over note-learning, tone production, posture, and other things associated with singing. Each year we begin all the way at the beginning of each category because we found that kids were forgetting concepts learned the year before. This system of objectives structures much of what we do. I am a firm believer in the thought that the more you know about something, the more you can love it.

Third: I teach a lot of history through the music we sing. If we're going to do Brahms, I want them to know what in the Sam Hill is going on in his life and his times. We talk a lot about composers and arrangers, because it just is so necessary that they leave with that knowledge. I also teach a lot of theory, but not with a text or anything. We compose. Each one is responsible for composing and recording, using a keyboard, a simple one-line melody by the end of the year. Things like melody line and key signatures and time signatures can all be learned by using them to compose. And keyboard. And we listen: the kids I have now have heard Thomas Hampson, a baritone; they've heard Domingo; they've heard the Bulgarian Women's Chorus, because of their unique sound. Before they leave me, they will listen to all types of voices and choirs. I end up teaching voice on the basis of what they've heard. I think listening is very important.

Fifth: To me, there is something more important than for the kids to sing beautifully, and that is what I teach. To make the kids feel good about themselves. We can teach morality. We can teach respect for others. And we can teach the kids to feel good about themselves. I have encountered so many kids that have such low self esteem, and music can be a vehicle to help all of that. Seeing a student gain confidence and respect for themselves is so wonderful. It's the most important reason I teach. Is there anything else, anything academic that you try to teach? I don't spend a lot of time with specific lessons. I try to make the kids aware of history as it applies to the music we are singing. I also try to teach kids that all music is good music if it is performed well.

D. Important Related Topics

1. The Boy's Changing Voice

First Respondent: First of all you need to find out what the boy's voice is like — what is its quality, what is its range? Then you put him on the part which most closely matches his capabilities. The high voices sing first tenor if they are capable of it, and if that is too low, you create a part for them. It should be dealt with as a natural phenomenon, not as an oddity.

Second: There is no question that at the young end of our student population there are voice changes taking place in both the boys and the girls. The girls are easier to handle because their voice change is for the most part a change in quality, not in range. So there is less drama involved. I basically ignore talk of register changes because I don't want to introduce problems where none may exist. With the men's voices, I just keep them singing. If they have a three-note range, we sing those three good notes. If they still have voices in the female range, I have them sing as much of the tenor part as possible because I think that putting these boys in the girls' sections can severely affect their enjoyment and cause a lot of embarrassment. I just check a lot to make sure they are not pushing the lower tones.

Third: I don't know if you'll believe this, but I have never had a boy with an unchanged voice in my choir. I'm not sure why. Do the kids from some of the non-Western cultures physically develop faster? Sounds like a Ph.D. dissertation to me. I really think they just stay away from choir until it's over.

Fourth: Since I am an instrumentalist, I don't know much about vocal pedagogy. I basically leave the voice alone and let time provide a solution. I often write a part with the most comfortable portions of both the tenor and the alto so that there will be a separate part for the boys. I try not to have them sing girls' parts.

Fifth: I run into that a lot. First of all I try to make sure that those boys whose voices haven't changed feel good about them-selves. That's the first thing I do. I try to pick literature that makes these guys feel good, even if they are singing up an octave. We sing a lot in falsetto, which makes these guys feel good because they haven't yet lost that voice up there. By the way, to help the boys who have forgotten their high voices to use falsetto, I go back to some of the old be-bop stuff, the Beach Boys, any of those old groups. That's also the big reason I want to isolate the boys that age from the girls, because we can work on voices more effectively. One thing I like to do is to have all the boys sing the high parts in a song. The ones with unchanged voices really feel good when they can do something the other guys have trouble doing.

Sixth: Since good tenors are so hard to come by, I use those boys whose voices haven't changed yet as tenors. They have often been the salvation of that section. It's important not to push the voice too low.

Seventh: I doubt that I have anything to add to what you have already collected. I believe it is important to keep singing through the voice change, and that is most easily effected when boys meet in their own rehearsal (at least part of the time), and I am able to give a lot of one-to-one instruction. I write parts that fit the voices I have, and I will go to all lengths to avoid bruising tender egos by having boys sing with a female section.

2. Singing in Foreign Languages

First Respondent: It depends on the level of the group. I think with the beginning groups, even, it would probably be important for them to sing, I guess, in Latin—because of the great volume of good music, educationally speaking. I think as the groups advance, it is important to introduce other languages. It is important to sing in, say, Spanish, and the other Romance languages. If I run into a piece in a language I'm not familiar with, I'd not hesitate to bring in the foreign language teachers to help.

Second: I believe in singing in a number of languages so that students can get used to hearing the works of a composer the way he wrote them. I use English first as an introduction to Latin and Italian. Hebrew and German are just one step further, with a different set of consonants. When I get into languages I am not fluent in pronouncing, such as French or Russian, I get the foreign language teachers to come down and teach the languages. The kids get a kick out of seeing their language teachers in a new setting. I think it is important that you know your community to know what languages they would like their kids to sing in, maybe Polish or Russian or even the Scandinavian languages.

Third: I tend to stay away from things with texts you can't understand; I think that is due to much of my training, when teachers listened to a work in Latin and asked, "Why?" I see the beauty of singing in the original language, but it is so much more beautiful if you can understand it. You know what I mean? But, of course, my choirs sing a little in languages: Latin comes first because of the similarity of many vowel and consonant sounds to those in English; a logical transition from Latin is to Hebrew because many of those vowel sounds are similar. I kind of like French because I have had an extensive background in it. But mainly we sing texts we can understand and relate to. You can sing a line so much more beautifully when you know what it is trying to say.

Fourth: I have used Latin more than any other foreign language. Beyond that I have not done a lot with languages. I don't do much of that except for contest pieces.

Fifth: I do very little music in foreign languages any more because I found myself teaching the concepts of diction, but losing the meaning of the text. It was a case of not being able to see the forest for the trees. I want expressive singing based on the meaning of the text of the music, and I lost much of that in my quest for correct pronunciation.

Sixth: I don't use foreign languages in my show choirs, but I may use Latin in my training groups so they can have the experience of needing to understand a text not in their own language.

Seventh: I really do very little singing that is not English. When I do venture forth, it is in solo singing in Italian. When I prioritize the goals of my program, foreign languages are not at the top.

3. Popular Choral Music

First Respondent: First of all, I think that the whole program of music should offer the students the opportunity to explore every genre of music. I think kids should do jazz, and experience scat singing. I think the literature of the Broadway shows can be used. There are some wonderful arrangements available of some of that music.

Second: I use some popular music in my concert groups because the kids want to do it. I find that Broadway music and songs from the '50s and '60s translate best into choral arrangements. The pop music of recent years, being mainly solo in nature and far less melody-oriented translates very poorly into usable choral arrangements, even though many of our publishers keep giving us more like that every year. With my show choir (which I firmly believe should not be a part of the choral curriculum) I do several choreographed numbers because the audience loves those numbers. Be careful that you choose music that is suitable for the group that is performing it. Because I have little background in performing or preparing gospel music, I often bring in someone to help me— someone with a knowledge of the sound and style necessary for an accurate performance.

Third: I'm a snob. I've told you that already. There's just so much "pop poop" out there that I just don't buy it unless it just reaches out and grabs me. I do more tunes from musicals and novelties. [Interviewer: Vocal jazz?] Some. There's just as much trash in vocal jazz, but every once in a while you run across a real gem, and when I find one I may use it in choir. One of the problems is that I don't know as much about it as I need to. Again, I would go for a piece because of its lyric; maybe it works in a theme. That's about the only time I use pop in my curricular choir.

Fifth: I have no problem using it, but I think it is important not to go overboard. I like to do medleys from musicals, and with the exception of rap, I am open to almost all styles. I don't allow groups like jazz choirs and especially show choirs to be included in the daily curriculum; they can get so power-crazy and they are capable of becoming the tail that wags the dog. The kids get fanatical about winning, and when the parents who are involved also get fanatical, they can start trying to be decision-makers, and they try to run things, which is my job. Gospel? I will tell you that I disapprove of what I hear coming from the schools that have these groups. There is no concept of tone production; everything is shouted in the name of style. But I don't have a problem using all of these types of pop music in my concert choirs. We usually do one pops concert every year, and it is very popular. But everything we sing, we sing with integrity. That's very important.

Sixth: Contemporary styles, and all that their performance includes — choreography, feature dancing, costumes, instrumental groups — are at the heart of my program. I think it is very important that students learn the art of entertainment, not just the art of singing.

Seventh: Yes; I love pop-style music. My background is filled with show tunes, musicals, and jazz. Choreography is also a major interest of mine. Having said that, I feel that pop music should be included in a choral program to provide a balance with the more standard choral literature. I believe you need to look HARD for good arrangements; the market is flooded with bad pop charts every fall. I also feel like the music I choose needs to fit — with the choir's interests, and with my strengths.

E. The Extracurricular Program

1. So You Are Going to Do a Musical

First Respondent: The first thing to do is to call someone in your area who knows his away around musicals and learn from him or her. Know what resources you have available. You might think of doing a smaller show at first, like a *Charlie Brown,* or if you are more ambitious, maybe *The Fantasticks*. And I would always bring in other people to help. That way you have a larger pool of experience and knowledge to draw on.

Second: I think a musical is an important part of the school music program. If I were to give advice to a young teacher, I would tell her to pick an easy show, know your talent, and get lots of help. Although all shows have things about them that are hard, there are shows that are easier than others. Look at small cast shows and shows from the "golden age" of musicals. By knowing your talent, I mean that it is important to know that you have talent to cover each role. It is not necessary to have a single person in mind for the role. And finally, tap your faculty, your parents, and the community talent to put together a team to run the show. It is too big a job for one person.

Third: Oh, I'm the wrong person to ask. I want to control every facet of the production so that in the end I can say the production is my product. [Interviewer: What would you tell a young teacher with no experience in putting on shows?] Get help!

Fifth: To a young teacher I would say, once again, go out and get help. Get outside the walls of the school; go out and find somebody you respect for each of the various jobs. If you can find people who are teachers, that's fine, but don't be afraid to get someone who knows what he is doing who is not associated with the school. But I want to retain control and be the leader—for two reasons. First of all I am bossy, and second, I want the music not to suffer at the hands of someone who doesn't know how to control or direct singers.

Sixth: Essentially, every show I do with my show choir is a small Broadway-style performance. When I do include a musical in my yearly agenda, I pick one that fits the talent I have. Because of my own limitations, I get as much free help or as much as the budget will allow. I tend to choose a show that is more recent than the classics like *Brigadoon*. Some of our recent productions have been *Jesus Christ Superstar* and *Pippin*. My most important advice for a young teacher is to plan every minute of every rehearsal. Don't leave anything to chance.

Seventh: Now you're hitting me where I live. I love to do

shows—I have since I performed in high school. And, yes, I do have some suggestions. First of all, don't try to do every aspect of the show yourself. Tap the talent of your faculty, the community, and even the students. Some of the jobs that need to be covered by assistants are:

> Stage director
> Dance captain or choreographer
> Production director
> Stage manager/designer
> Costumer

There are others that can be included, and be aware that a number of the jobs can be consolidated into one, depending on the strength of your "volunteers." Be very careful when you choose a show; doing the wrong one can spell failure regardless of the talent of the kids and the adults. Also, make sure that the contents and story lines are acceptable by your community's standards. But don't forget that our role is two-pronged; to develop the abilities of our students and to create a more intelligent consumer (the audience).

2. Travel, Parent Groups, and Competition

First Respondent: It's important to have the parents involved in supervising the groups when the conductor is not available, and that is one reason I feel like parent groups are important. They will also be instrumental in travel, which, I believe, can be a *wonderful* experience, depending on the level of the program. You have the opportunity to perform the literature you have prepared several times, and that gives the kids an opportunity to grow more than when they prepare a concert and sing it only once. I think a great idea is to take your choir back to the college you attended and let the students clinic with them. What about competitions? No. Unless you are in a high-powered community that would respond positively to you bringing home a three-foot trophy.

Second: Parent organizations are GREAT! They take the load off the shoulders of the choral director in so many different ways. They can run fundraisers; they can be or supply chaperons for concerts; they can put together social events for the singers, and they can be support for the teacher. It is true that they can get out of hand, but it is the director's job to make sure that doesn't happen — plain and simple. Travel is a broadening experience, and I have found that my choirs "gel" while preparing for and taking a trip. Our favorite kind of trip is to arrange a visit with a college at which we are clinic-ed by a faculty member; we perform at a convocation or for their music ed. classes, then we make our choir available to their conducting students or methods students to provide them a "live" high school choir to work with. What a great experience that can be; and it can be the focal point for a multi-overnight trip or for a day trip within the state. As far as competitions are concerned, I generally am not interested in them because I don't feel that the judges are always good enough. I don't want to spend a lot of the choral parents' money to read or hear, "Good job. Keep singing." I would like to take part in one of those swing choir competitions, but I don't because we don't do the style of performance that seems to be in vogue right now. Also, I don't believe in putting my show choir in the curriculum, so the amount of time available for rehearsal is seriously compromised. I have a real problem philosophically with a student being able to experience any show choir music during the school day.

Third: I used to always say "nay" to competition. It always boils down to who's sitting in judgment and how they got there. I'd say about 50 percent of them don't say anything more substantial than "they look pretty, and don't they sing well together." I'd just like to throttle them because I do a lot of judging, and I know better. I like the festival idea where the kids sing without being judged more than the competition. Although I inherited a situation where the kids were used to, "let's go to this place and buy a trophy and come home." I know the kids and the parents like those trophies, but I wonder if it's worth seeing the kids' faces when they don't win. As far as parents, I just love the parents involved in my program. They help me with so many things at concert time and throughout the year. I couldn't do without them. And as far as travel, we only travel as a complete department; that's a school rule. So our options are kind of limited.

Fourth: None of our musical groups travel. The one exception to that is when we go to state choir contests. We do have parent groups to raise money for choir banquets and awards and almost anything else the choir needs money for.

Fifth: I love traveling with kids. But I always made sure I had the right kind of and enough chaperons that I didn't have to spend my time on discipline. If I came into it, somebody was going home. Papers were signed by parents before we left, and everyone knew the rules: a serious infraction of the rules and the student went home at the parents' expense.

I guess I have addressed the question of my attitude toward parent groups already. I rely very heavily upon the parents, even though I make it very clear that I need to control what the choir should sing and do and where they should go. Their job is to assist me in meeting these goals. I have seen a lot of parent groups that got way out of hand—parents wanting a say even in curricular matters. No! No! No!

I don't even know where to start with competition. I've judged many a contest in my day—especially swing choir. And I used to take part in some of them. I think competition can provide a good incentive for the kids to work hard toward a specific goal. But in my opinion we have gone crazy. We have created monsters with them. Also, I think we are teaching kids very bad messages—to stab your mother to win a trophy. And I think we are doing music education a disservice.

Sixth: Competition is a major part of my program; competition demands travel, and travel needs money, creating the necessity for a parent group to raise funds. I am a strong supporter of all three. Contrary to the feelings of many of my peers, I believe that competition sharpens skills, creates camaraderie, and heightens self-esteem. And I believe the experience of travel is invaluable in broadening the horizons, especially of those students who don't normally have that opportunity. Finally, I could not do my job if it weren't for the choir parents who take over so many responsibilities and leave me free to work on the show. I've heard many stories of such groups usurping too much power from the director, but I have never had that experience.

Seventh: I believe:

that competition can be a very important aspect of the choral program—if it is not over-emphasized;

that travel can be one of the best ancillary experiences we can offer
our students—as long as it doesn't become the ruler of my curriculum;

that parent groups are wonderful, and their effect on the program
can be very important—as long as they don't try to run the department and make decisions that are not theirs to make.

F. Non-Choral Concepts to Be Considered by a Choir Director

1. Preparing a Budget

First Respondent: I think it is important for you to impress upon
your administration the need to purchase x amount of new literature
each year, as well as other purchases for the department. I think it
is important to lay this out in advance and to justify these purchases
in terms of their usefulness. Evaluate everything in terms of program
goals so that they understand and don't have to ask you why that
is important.

Second: I am fortunate to live in a district where most of our
department's needs are met very nicely through the school budget.
But the reason I believe that most of my requests are approved is
that I am frugal. I use a great deal of music already in our school's
music library. I do only a few brand new charts each year to hold
down costs, and where I can legally do it, I prepare some arrangements for my choirs. A second key is to always prepare your requests
at least a year in advance so that you don't put people in the unen-
viable position of having to scour the school budget to accommodate your request. Be frugal. Plan in advance.

Fifth: I get a certain amount; I think it is $1000. They call it for
supplies, and I never use all of it. I end up pulling most of my stuff
from my basement or from my brain, you know. That $1000 is
mainly for music. If I need a piano tuned, the school does it. If I
need robes cleaned, the school does it. So I feel like I have all I

need. I never spend it all, but this year I am going to have to because the folders are just shredded. And I bought twenty-five red chef hats to do a novelty number at Christmas. My principal signs off on all my purchases, but I have never had him question anything I bought—so far.

Sixth: I am very fortunate. With the funds given to me by the school, plus the money raised by the parent group, I basically have enough money to run my program. Students are expected to buy their own costumes.

Seventh: I have always worked as a part of a music team that prepares one departmental budget. I submit my wants, fantasies, and true needs, and somebody up the financial chain makes decisions about how much money I get.

2. Preparing a Student for College Music Study

First Respondent: I think it is essential that you prepare a student for an audition, and you might want to verify that fact with their private teacher. You need to evaluate their sight-reading ability, because that will be part of the audition. They should have a variety of literature and languages represented in their program, and that depends on what degree they will be auditioning for. Generally, I would stick with the classics.

Second: I think it is my job to help match a student to what I know about the colleges he or she is considering; but as little as I know, I think I am his or her best resource. As far as auditions, most of our kids study voice privately, and their private teachers prepare their auditions with them.

Third: It doesn't happen very often. I say, "Can you do anything else and be happy? Do it!" If I do get a child who wants it, my main job is to offer a reality check. That there are 5,000 out there with equal talent. Do you have the drive and are your skills varied enough to sustain you? I give advice on colleges, and I write recs, lots of letters to schools. The counselors don't know, they just don't know. And that's all right that they don't know. I help the students pick music for an audition, and I have them pay an accompanist to rehearse with them and go to the audition with them.

Fourth: Help them find the college that is best for them, the one that suits them best; then, help them get ready for an audition. What else is there?

3. Music Professional Organizations

First Respondent: I think that membership in ACDA and MENC is absolutely essential. Get involved and attend their conventions. The reading sessions are, I think, the main reason to attend the conventions and exhibits of these organizations. Choral America is another one, but I do think ACDA and MENC are the two most essential.

Second: ACDA and MENC provide good reading sessions, and attending them is a good way to meet people and to get repertoire ideas. But remember, reading sessions sponsored by publishing companies are likely to be loaded with that company's latest releases. Be discriminating. I firmly believe that local and state conventions are more useful (at least for me) than the national and regional conventions.

Third: You need to network, need to network. I'm not sure they do anything for me other than provide a resource. Young teachers need to be involved with their local music ed. organizations, because that's where they can get the most. I like ACDA more than the others because they have better literature—their magazine articles are better. They are written for intelligent people, and I am a snob.

Fifth: I left professional organizations alone a long time ago, Walt. I just can't stand being around "hoity-toity" people. I quit going to conventions a long time ago as well. I didn't like the atmosphere: "We're doing the Brahms *Requiem*. What are you doing this year?" Naaaah! I think the original intentions behind professional organizations were good, but they have grown into something else.

Sixth: I support and belong to MENC for two reasons. I enjoy its journal, and I appreciate its support of contemporary choral music.

Seventh: I have been more involved with professional organizations in the past than I am now. It seems that (at least in the two organizations I support) the same topics keep being addressed, usually without a great deal of growth. I do take a lot of rehearsal materials from the literature available to me; I attend workshops sponsored by each; and I find a lot of interesting journal articles.

4. Why Should Music Be in the High School Curriculum?

First Respondent: There is a part of each one of us that involves our feelings, our taste, our hearts. I cannot touch these things, and no matter how hard some of my cohorts try, I cannot measure them. Giving students the chance to explore their relationship to these feelings is the purpose of the arts in the music curriculum. I cannot always show you the results of arts education on a student, but I can sure show you the results of the lack of it.

Second: Too many people approach this question in terms of "touchy feely" results. I have some very precise reasons that music should be in my school's curriculum:

The arts contribute to a well-rounded individual.
To experience, to feel, to create.
To lighten the load of a stressful school day.
To foster group cooperation.
And, undoubtedly, to provide the "touchy feely" component of a student's life.

Third: The arts enrich the soul.

Fifth: Music touches people in places that no other discipline can. It is our duty to make it possible for a student to live a richer life because of what we teach.

Sixth: Because it causes the student to experience energy, beauty, and sensitivity in a way no other discipline can.

Seventh: I could write a book on this topic, but in the interest of time (my husband and kids want dinner), I believe that the arts in general are important in a school curriculum because they are essential in developing a whole person.

G. Fifty Things No One Ever Told Me

First Respondent: I think your list is excellent.
  Second:
> You will need to be a therapist as well as teacher.
> You need to learn to handle raging parents.
> You will need to be a ticket office.

  Third:
> Don't drive a student anywhere in your private car.
> Don't go into the faculty lounge. I don't think that any-
> thing positive can come from an arena where the attitude
> is complaining and gossiping.
> Don't pass judgment. Who's to say whose voice is more
> beautiful or who is more talented?
> Every student is a potential original.
> Oh, I know; buy a piano that is low enough to see over.
> I am very short, and it is incredibly difficult to work with
> a group when you can't see the singers.

  Fifth: Nothing to add.
  Sixth: This seems to be an excellent list, but I would have real
problems sticking to all of them—like not giving kids rides home
after rehearsals, or not attending cast parties, and a number of others.
  Seventh: What a great idea! Here are my additions:
> Your students will give you exactly what you expect
> from them; if you ask for a lot, you will get a lot,
> and if you ask little, little is what you'll get.
> Less is more; work for quality; do not settle for quan-
> tity.
> Summer and holiday vacations are more than a luxury;
> they are absolutely necessary in the life of a teacher.

Appendix A

FORMS OFTEN USED

Letter to Assure Parental Support of Concert Attendance

Dear Choral Parent or Guardian:
Please take a moment to read this letter carefully and go through it with your son or daughter. It may represent a significant change from past practices. Each quarter of the school year we will present one concert, and all choirs will be represented. Attendance at that concert will be a big part of your son's or daughter's quarter grade; in fact, it is very similar to a quarter final exam in an academic course. Here are the dates of the concerts for which attendance is required:

October 24	An Evening of Music	in the GHS Auditorium at 7:30 p.m.
December 16	A Holiday Offering	in the GHS Rotunda at 3:00 p.m.
March 6	Festival of Music*	in the Auditorium of Juning HS at 3:00 p.m.
May 12	A Night on Broadway	in the GHS cafeteria at 7:00 p.m.

*This festival is a combination of singers from all six schools in our district. Transportation will be provided for all students for rehearsals and performance.

Please have your child sign along with your signature, showing that your family is committed to making sure your student will take part in all choral activities scheduled for this year.

Student signature_____

Parental Signature_____

Please remember to return this form to me by September 14.

Thanks a lot,

Walter Lamble

Choir Director, GHS

Sample Audition Form

To all GHS singers:

The purpose of this audition is for me to get to know you and your voice as I begin my teaching here at GHS. This information will help me place you in the choir I think best suits the two of us. Please fill in the following information and have it with you when you come in to sing for me. Do not write on the back.

Your Name_____

Your Address_____

_____

Your Phone Number_____

Your Year in School_____

What experience have you had in singing? (Choirs, solos, rock groups, any other)

_____

_____

_____

_____

_____

_____

What experience have you had in other types of musical activities? (Band, orchestra, private music lessons, plays, musicals, piano lessons, any other)

_____

_____

_____

_____

_____

What was your grade point average last semester?_____

If you've sung in choirs, what voice part did you sing? S A T B (Circle one)

Judging Sheet for Choral Auditions

Name_____

What song did he or she sing?_____

Ranges:

Highest to lowest   Best Sound

_____   _____

_____   _____

_____   _____

_____   _____

_____   _____

Description of sound (light, warm, breathy, forced, etc.)

_____

_____

_____

Problems (pitch, carries chest voice too high, strains for {high} {low} notes, vowel peculiarities, sound problems, etc.)

_____

_____

_____

Other notes_____

_____

Urgent note to a young teacher: TAKE YOUR TIME. Be thorough in your assessment and write details. This is important for you, so you can help the student with the vocal problems you hear; for the student, so he or she can work on problems you hear; and for parents who will want to have concrete reasons why their child did or did not make whatever the audition was for.

Choral Library Card File

NOTE: Make three copies of each of these cards for three separate files. 1. A file arranged by song title 2. A file arranged by voicing 3. A file arranged by style/occasion

Title of Song_____
File Number_____
Composer/Arranger/Editor_____
Publisher_____Publisher Number_____

Style/occasion: General Sacred   Christmas
                   General Secular   Hanukkah
                   Pop   Graduation
                   Jazz   Funeral
                   Spiritual   Contemporary, not popular
                   Gospel   Non-traditional
Difficulty level: Very easy
                   Easy
                   Medium difficulty
                   Difficult
                   Very difficult

Language (if other than English)_____
When added to library_____Cost at that time_____
Address of publisher_____

Date(s) performed _____ _____
                          _____ _____ _____
                          _____ _____ _____

Music Checkout Form

Name of Choir   *Concert Choir*
Student Name   **Title**   **Copy #**   **Returned**

_____

_____

_____

_____

_____

_____

_____

_____

_____

_____

_____

Appendix B

WARM-UP EXERCISES

For basic vocal warmup

For wider range warmup

For preparing legato passages

For preparing staccato phrases

Pa Pa Pa *Sim.*   Ha Ha Ho Ho Hoo Hoo He He Hey Hey Hoo Hoo He He Ha

Tongue Twister

Red   lea - ther   yel - low   lea - ther   Red   lea - ther   yel - low   lea - ther

Intonation practice

A great drill for internal rhythm

1.) Students sing as written
2.) Teacher calls out a number, students leave a hole where that number was
3.) Continue until all 10 numbers have been called and students are counting in their heads

1   2   3   4   5   6   7   8   9   10   1   2   3   5   6   7   8   9   10

Appendix C

MUSIC LENDING LIBRARIES

Tams-Witmark
560 Lexington Ave.
New York, NY 10022
Phone: 212-688-2525
Fax: 800-826-7121

Music Theatre International
421 West 54th St.
New York, NY 10019
Phone: 212-541-4684
Fax: 212-397-4684
E-mail: licensing@mtishows.com

Samuel French, Inc.
45 West 25th St.
New York, NY 10010
Phone: 212-206-8125
Fax: 212-206-1429

Rodgers and Hammerstein Theatre Library
229 West 28th St., 11th Floor
New York, NY 10001
Phone: 212-564-4000
Fax: 212-268-1245

Appendix D

TIMELINES FOR PRODUCING A MUSICAL

Six-Month Timeline

Six-Month Timeline for Producing a Musical

	Month 1	Month 2	Month 3	Month 4	Month 5	Month 6
Director and Staff	Peruse material ordered Study scripts and scores	Study scripts and scores	Choose show Study script and score Sign contract Produce preliminary budget	Prepare for auditions and rehearsals	Hold auditions Cast show Begin rehearsals	Continue rehearsals Production week (See below)
Committee Chairs	Assist director **if asked**	Assist director **if asked**	Study budget needs		All committees working	All committees working Production week (See below)
Producer			Study show	Announce show and auditions Prepare and make available audition material Design publicity material	Announce cast Begin publicity campaign Get tickets printed, Distribute rehearsal material Arrange rehearsal schedule with all directors Arrange rehearsal spaces	Publicity campaign begins Newspaper publicity Tickets go on sale Production week (See below)

Choreographer		Study show Begin to design choreography	Design choreography	Begin teaching choreography	Rehearse Be ready to polish Production week (See below)
Technical Director		Study show Begin to design set, lights, and sound	Designing set, lights, and sound	Build set Finish light and sound plots	Finish building Tentative lighting and sound plots finished Production week (See below)
Musical Director	Study scores	Study score	Learn score	Rehearse score with singers Choose orchestra members Begin instrumental rehearsals	Polish vocals Work on orchestra Production week (See below)
Costumer		Study show Meet with Director and Tech Director Begin to design costumes	Design costumes	Build costumes Order rental costumes	Building costumes Initial fittings for leads Production week (See below)
Cast			Prepare to audition	Rehearsals	In rehearsals Production week (See below)

Final Rehearsals Timeline

There is no magic to the information listed below. It is a system which worked well for my staff and me.

10th day before opening	Music only—orchestra and cast in music room
9th day before opening	Second music day—add dances for a complete musical run
8th day before opening	Workthrough of Act I—orchestra in pit—no tech
7th day before opening	Workthrough of Act II—orchestra in pit—no tech
6th day before opening	"Dry tech"—jump cue to cue to set lights and sound Minimal cast involvement—no pit musicians. Could be a very long night for the directors and the tech crew.
5th day before opening	1. A complete tech workthrough—lights, sound, and set, musicians in pit, difficult costume changes 2. Runthrough of entire show with all components in place. Because of its length, this rehearsal must be on a weekend.
4th day before opening	Act I—all forces—workthrough (twice, if possible)
3rd day before opening	Act II—all forces—workthrough (twice, if possible)
The two nights before opening	Dress rehearsals—show conditions
The day after closing	Return to school with tools to strike the set.

Appendix E

A BUDGET TEMPLATE

Monies Requested for the Choral Music Area

Supplies	**$1,100**	
New Music		$600
40 choral folios @$4.25		170
District and All-State Expenses		330
		$1,100
Equipment	**$1,000**	
2 sets, finger cymbals	@$60	$120
2 piano benches	@$175	350
1 choral folio cabinet		450
		$920
Books	**$300**	
1 set, foreign pronunciation guides		$200
1 annual installment of Grove Dictionary		100
		$300
Non-Print Materials	**$200**	
Assorted CDs		$200
Costumes	**$400**	
4 replacement robes	@$100	$400
Repairs	**$500**	
4 piano tuning	@$75	$300
Robe repair		200
		$500
Software	**$300**	
Assorted software		$300
Audio-Visual Equipment	**$275**	
1 Double cassette recorder		$175
1 Camcorder		100
		$275
Periodicals	**$100**	
Daily newspaper		$35
Electronic Musician		65
		$100
TOTAL REGULAR BUDGET	**$4,175**	

Note: Special high-priced items are requested of and approved/denied by a special budget committee.

WALTER LAMBLE is a retired choral educator with over thirty years' experience in the classroom. He has a Ph.D. in music education from the University of Iowa.